InformationDesignWorkbook

ROCKPORT

"Clutter is a failure of design, not an attribute of information."

—Edward Tufte

First published in the United States of America by Rockport Publishers, a member of Quayside Publishing Group
100 Cummings Center
Suite 406-L
Beverly, Massachusetts 01915-6101
Telephone: (978) 282-9590
Fax: (978) 283-2742
www.rockpub.com

Library of Congress Cataloging-in-Publication Data
Baer, Kim.
  Information design workbook: graphic approaches, solutions, and inspiration + 30 case studies / Kim Baer.
     p.   cm.
  ISBN 1-59253-410-4
  1. Communication in design. 2. Graphic arts.
  3. Design–Human factors. 4. Visual communication.
  5. Interactive multimedia–Design. I. Title.

NC997.B24 2008
741.6–dc22
2007039179

ISBN-13: 978-1-59253-627-6
ISBN-10: 1-59253-627-1

10 9 8 7 6 5

Design: KBDA

Printed in China

InformationDesignWorkbook

GRAPHIC APPROACHES, SOLUTIONS, AND INSPIRATION + 30 CASE STUDIES

ROCKPORT PUBLISHERS

Kim Baer with contributing writer Jill Vacarra

CONTENTS

The Fundamentals. An overview of
the discipline, plus an in-depth look
at processes and tools.

Case Studies. Information design highlights and in-depth interviews with leading designers in the field.

Preface

If you've ever been lost in a parking structure, searching in vain for your car, then you know the power of design. If you've ever walked into the ladies' room when, in fact, you're a man ("That icon on the door sure looked male to me!"), then you know the power of design. If you've ever cast your vote for one candidate only to find it tallied to another, then you know the power of design. Design can confuse. Design can mislead. Design can change the course of history.

MORE THAN A TOOL TO TEMPT THE EYE

Design can clarify and simplify. It can inspire loyalty, sell millions, or save lives.
The power of design lies in its nuance: Intelligently planned and skillfully achieved,
it is more than a tool to tempt the eye. It's the difference between considered and
purchased, annoyed and inspired, lost and found.

AN AMAZING TIME TO BE A DESIGNER

The importance of design is more acknowledged than ever, even in the general press.
However, a good deal of this focus has been on product design. What may be less celebrated
are the thousands of ways we depend on design to help us sort through complicated information and complex choices. Whether the information is online, printed, environmental, or
experiential, the key is to craft the experience for the audience and look for ways in which
design can cut through the clutter to the essence of an idea.

Over the years, clients have typically turned to designers to solve problems and devise smart
design and communications solutions. Today's world of information overload means that
designers are frequently asked to distill and simplify massive quantities of information. In
terms of the designer's evolving role in business, expertise in information design has become
a key factor in providing value to clients.

NEW WAYS OF THINKING

In the past, graphic designers were not specifically trained how to approach the design of
information-intensive projects, or think of design from a user-centric approach. Both of these
tasks can seem challenging, even daunting. Our hope is that this book will make both the
idea and the practice of information design appealing and approachable.

THIS BOOK:

- Leads you through the mindset and kind of thinking
  that support good information design

- Gives you an overview of the types of processes and
  tools you can use to create effective information design

- Shows real-world examples of successful projects

- Presents interviews with some of the premier
  practitioners working in the field today

A USER-CENTRIC MINDSET

An information designer who's in the zone
is likely to have the following traits:

- A passion for asking questions

- A keen eye for detail

- Respect for the end-user's time and needs

- The ability to see the forest <u>and</u> the trees

- A sensitivity to everyday annoyances

- The empathy to imagine what others feel

- The ability to observe and participate
  at the same time

- A sense of humor—when isn't this a
  useful trait?

The following anecdotes will give you a
sense for how to think like an information
designer. These are real-world stories from
the trenches, detailing the various ways
user experiences could be improved if seen
with a user-centric design mindset. Once
you have the user-centric mindset, you'll
never see the world the same way again.

GUERILLA PUBLIC SERVICE

Due to the lack of adequate signage
at the busy junction of the 110 and
Interstate 5 freeways near downtown
Los Angeles, motorists were constantly
missing their interchange and getting
lost. In 2001, artist Richard Ankrom got
fed up and created completely realistic
freeway and directional signage to
correct the problem. Ankrom's precisely
reproduced guide signs were so realistic
that the California Department of Transportation assumed it was an "inside
job" until the artist revealed the stunt
nine months later in a news article.

CURSING IN THE AISLES

"If you make a visit to your office supply store on any given day, you're likely to find several customers agonizing over the sea of confusing items in the ink cartridge replacement aisle. An information design nightmare, ink packaging is often designed with the same template. Many inks serve multiple printers. To find the right one, you have to scan assorted, hard-to-pinpoint printer numbers on the same small box. Is that image of the parrot on the package relevant, part of an image coding system? Next time the ink runs out, you too will be cursing in the ink aisles." —Ann Enkoji

YOUR CAR IS WAITING. SOMEWHERE.

"Ever lose your car in a parking deck? The problem of multistory parking structures is an issue worldwide. Very few parking structures create vista icons or prompts to help those of us with short memories and stressed circumstances remember where we parked. Parking structures are clearly created by engineers for car storage purposes and not for car users who wish to continue a relationship with their vehicle." —Tania Konishi

I'M SORRY, CAN YOU REPEAT THAT?

"We were standing in a long customs line that was taking forever and I came to realize that it was because the customs agent (decked out in a giant cowboy hat and gold collar medallions) was giving directions (the identical directions, we might add) to each person in line as to how to get to their gate. And a good thing too, because I've never seen such bad/inadequate signage in an airport. That delay prevented our luggage from getting on the flight, but that's another story." —Barbara Cooper

CUSTOMER SERVICE

"Translation: Ignore the customer at all costs. All of my health insurance claims were being denied. Twenty-one calls later (not including the multiple automated phone system runarounds), I had a new excuse from each representative: computer error, misspelled name, incorrect ID number, wrong zip code, no record of me as a client. No rep would give a name, so there was zero accountability. I asked to speak to a supervisor. The person I spoke to pretended to be a supervisor and gave a false name. I wrote a letter and sent it to several company locations and copied the state attorney general's office. I filed thirty written appeals. Eventually the claims were just paid. No one ever explained the problem." —Diane Vacarra

AUTOMATIC WASTEFULNESS

"Automatic public restroom functionality: Wave of the future? Key to cleanliness? Sensors need to be carefully placed and calibrated, though, to ensure a good user experience. How much water is wasted by all those overly sensitive automatic systems that flush the toilet three times before you exit the stall? (Of course, unflushed toilets aren't desirable either.) How about when you soap up your hands with an automatic soap dispenser, but the automatic water faucet sensor pretends you're not there? Or when the automatic paper towel dispenser sensor is placed dangerously close to the sink, so that every time you lean over to wash your hands, wasteful reams of paper are unintentionally released?" —Leslie Lewis

WHERE'S THE @#!* ARTICLE?

"The information design in magazines often drives me nuts. A cover treatment sometimes promotes a juicy article topic that's nearly impossible to find inside the magazine. You flip through the pages like mad and you still can't find it. Finally you scour the table of contents. You think you've found the article buried somewhere in the magazine, but it has a completely different title. And it's really more of a blurb than a full-blown article. And sometimes the topic is only marginally related to the cover promotion. The information design equivalent of bait and switch!" —Jill Vacarra

ASSEMBLY AND LIFT-OFF?

"A couple of years ago I decided to make margaritas, so I bought a blender and then tried to put it together. It came with a wordless diagram with vague pictures of parts that joined together. The end result is that the margaritas went flying as the force of the motor blew apart the various parts of the blender that I clearly hadn't put together properly. That's when I learned to love beer." —Julie Zirbel

WHAT FLOOR, PLEASE?

"I'm constantly annoyed by the total lack of standards around information design for elevators and floor naming in the U.S. It would be so great if someone would think about making the signs outside the elevator match the buttons inside. In Germany, for instance, every elevator in every building is the same. Here, they sometimes indicate ground floor with a G (is that for 'ground' or 'garage'?). Floor one is sometimes the ground floor and sometimes the second story up. P? Is that for 'plaza' or 'parking'? It's particularly confusing when the building has entrances at different grades and the parking garage is partly above and partly below grade." —Chris V. Cho

Information design has been in existence as a discipline for many years, but the field is experiencing an exciting tipping point and is becoming a much more important aspect of every designer's practice. At the heart of the conversation: How can design help people navigate an increasingly complex landscape of messaging and data?

ABOUT INFORMATION DESIGN

1

What Is Information Design?

THERE IS SOME CONSENSUS

In the world of graphic design, information design is just coming into its own. The term is relatively recent and the subject of considerable debate in the design community. There are dozens of websites, blogs, special interest groups, and conferences all seeking to define the term.

Definitions and debate aside, there is some commonality in all the discussions about information design. Our current favorite definition comes from the Society for Technical Communication's (STC) special interest group for information design, which describes the discipline as "...the translating [of] complex, unorganized, or unstructured data into valuable, meaningful information."

Who Practices Information Design? One way to define a discipline is to look at its practitioners. Information design is practiced by a variety of professionals in various settings, working on many different types of projects, ranging from print to online

to environmental to experiential design. Not surprisingly, people are beginning to consider the term to be an umbrella or integrator for a host of other related disciplines, such as graphic design, information architecture, interaction design, usability engineering, human-computer interaction, human factors, writing, editing, and library sciences.

Specialists and Generalists. Some practitioners of information design are specialists and practice deeply in one aspect of the field, such as information architecture for websites, or usability research and testing. Some people focus on one type of information design such as simplification of forms, or wayfinding in the transportation field. In the past, information design has been the realm of specialists. However, it has become an increasingly important part of all design projects. Even general practitioners of design need to consider thinking about each of their projects in a user-centric way. The more complex the information is for a project, the greater the need for an information design process and mindset.

Root of the Matter. Sometimes it helps to understand a term by dissecting it. Let's take apart the term information design. Information on its own and without structure is likely to be just a jumble of data. Data can include words, pictures, movement, sound—basically anything a

A complex screen-based exhibit gives young museum visitors a chance to explore multiple levels of information. (See case study on page 180.)
Second Story Interactive Studios

"**Egyptian scribes sat every day in the marketplace and wrote hieroglyphic letters, reports, memos and proposals for their clients. At least since then, the business of assisting others to make their communications more effective has flourished.**" —Robert E. Horn

human being's senses can absorb and translate into meaning. If you add the word design to the equation, you add purpose and a plan. There's someone (the designer) trying to communicate that purpose and plan to create meaning for someone else (the audience).

Human beings have myriad ways of absorbing and understanding information, so designers must use numerous tactics and methods to make information meaningful. That's where the interdisciplinary part of information design comes into play. Writing, editing, graphics, and illustration all have their place in the practice of information design, as do research and testing of your ideas on potential audiences so you can make sure you're making the right choices and not just guessing.

Bottom line: All of these elements and tactics working together can help ensure the effective communication of information. Effective communication is the very essence of information design.

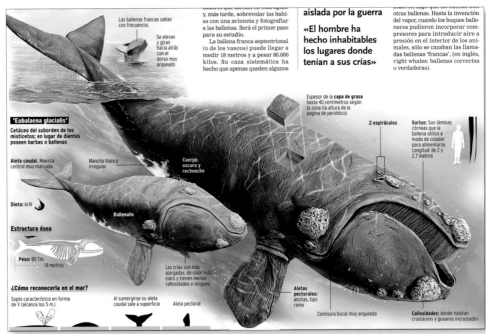

Research has shown that reader comprehension is enhanced when designers combine both visual and text-based cues.
Fernando Gómez Baptista

Related Fields

The following is a list of some of the disciplines that are related to the field of information design. Here we've tried to provide a brief description of each job type, as well as give a sense of how each discipline relates to the overall practice of information design. Since the field and corresponding list of roles and job titles are still in the process of being defined, titles, in some cases, may seem to duplicate each other or feature considerable overlap.

Graphic Designer: A graphic designer creates visual communications using text and images. With information design, the graphic designer uses color, symbols, type, and imagery, and makes deliberate aesthetic and cognitive choices to create effective communications. (See Chapter 4 for examples of how the graphic designer's toolkit applies to information design.)

Information Architect: An information architect (IA) organizes and categorizes information. This can include creating classification schemes and nomenclature for websites, software, or other applications for both online and real world environments.

The IA is often heavily involved in the planning of information design projects, creating high-level documentation of project structure, and conducting usability analysis and testing. (See Chapters 2 and 3 for detailed descriptions of IA process, documentation, and testing.)

Interaction Designer: An interaction designer works to define and create the specific behavior of features and systems where users interact online, or with software, for products, devices, environments, and services. An interaction designer considers how the user actually manipulates the features of a design (buttons, menus, slider bars, on/off switches, etc.), as well as the system's response to user input. While it's true that interaction designers are most often found working on websites, on software applications, or in the product design field, the interaction design thought process can come in handy when dealing with information design projects as diverse as how a traveler manages to unfold a map, or how a museum visitor might physically engage with exhibit content.

"There is nothing natural about information. Information, no matter what it is called—data, knowledge, or fact, song, story or metaphor—has always been designed." —Brenda Dervin

User Experience Designer: User experience (often referred to as UX) describes the overall experience and satisfaction level someone has when engaging with a service, product, or system. User experience is typically associated with taking the user-centric approach to design. The UX field is multidisciplinary and overlaps with or encompasses many other information design-related fields. Thus, the term "user experience designer" is a bit of a catch-all and could be used as an umbrella term to describe any of the following jobs when paired with a user-centric mindset: information architect, graphic designer, interface designer, usability specialist, or human-computer interaction specialist. All of these disciplines fall within the UX realm.

Usability Specialist: A usability specialist works from an acutely user-centric mindset. Usability specialists conduct usability testing and research, and study user behavior to learn from the patterns that emerge. For information design projects, the research that is gained from usability testing can inform and shape the design process. (See Chapter 3 for more detail on usability testing philosophy and practices.)

Human Factors Specialist: Human factors (also known as ergonomics) is a broad area of concern focused on the study of how humans behave in reaction to specific products, services, or environments. Human factors specialists pay special attention to human physical and cognitive capabilities and limitations in relation to work processes, and physical interaction with equipment or machinery. Usability research, which can play such a key part in creating targeted and useful information design, is related to, and has its roots in, the human factors discipline.

Human-Computer Interaction Specialist: Also referred to as HCI, human-computer interaction is the study of the interaction between humans and computers. Like many of the fields related to information design, HCI is interdisciplinary and focuses on a number of areas, including the design of computer software, hardware, and peripherals. HCI specialists apply design methodologies to real-world computer-related issues. Their work often revolves around designing graphical user interfaces. Any information design project that includes a human-computer relationship might benefit from the HCI mindset. For instance, if you're creating screen-based information design, you may want to factor in the types of devices that people will use to view it, from the perspective of the size and location of the device, the environment, and user interaction with that device.

Plain Language Expert: Specialists in plain language approach the text of any project from a user-centric mindset. Their focus is on particular audience needs. Characteristics of plain language writing include the use of short sentences, active voice, and headings to create structure and easier readability, and the omission of all unnecessary words. As proponents of clear organization and design of information, plain language experts make excellent collaborators for information design projects.

INFORMATION DESIGN IS UBIQUITOUS

Where do we see information design? It's all around us. General categories of information design have been defined for the purpose of this book as printed matter, information graphics, interactive, environmental, and experimental design. Following are some of the many situations where information design is found (and this list is just the tip of the iceberg):

- Roadway signage when you're driving

- The map you use to plan your journey

- The simplest brochure for a product or service

- Every website you've ever visited

- Instructions on your prescription bottle

- Every form you've ever filled out

- Automated phone systems for everything from movie listings to credit card balances

- Ballots and voter information guides

- New product assembly and usage guides for toys, furniture, and the latest gadgets

- Exhibits at museums, science centers, libraries, and other cultural destinations

- Every book you've ever read, from your math textbook to the phone book

- Signage for travel hubs such as airports and train terminals

MORE VALUABLE BY THE DAY

Just as time and pressure can make diamonds out of carbon, forces in our culture at large are shaping the notion of information design as a valued discipline. Some of these influences include:

Information Overload: Not Just Hype.
Did you know:

- Globally, there are more than 3,000 books published daily.

- There are 540,000 words in the English language today, more than five times as many as during Shakespeare's time.

- It is estimated that a week's worth of the *New York Times* contains more information than a person was likely to come across in a lifetime in the 18th century.

This collage of typical New York City parking signs showcases how confusing public signage can be. (See case study on page 132.)
Photo source: Addison

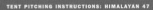

TENT PITCHING INSTRUCTIONS: HIMALAYAN 47

1

EN Remove components from the bag.
FR Retirez les différents éléments de la housse de transport.
DE Nehmen Sie die Einzelteile aus dem Zeltsack.

2

EN Lay the canopy out flat.
FR Mettez à plat la tente intérieure.
DE Breiten Sie das Innenzelt flach aus.

3

EN Carefully assemble each of the poles.
FR Assemblez minutieusement chacun des arceaux.
DE Stecken Sie vorsichtig alle Stangen zusammen.

4

EN Match pole color with trim at end of each sleeve and feed poles through sleeves.
FR Insérez et faites glisser les arceaux dans les fourreaux en respectant les couleurs.
DE Bringen Sie die Stangenfarbe mit der Farbe des Saums am jeweiligen Kanal in Übereinstimmung, und schieben Sie die Zeltstangen durch die Kanäle.

5

EN Push poles through sleeves and insert end of each pole into corresponding grommet.
FR Faites glisser les arceaux dans les fourreaux et insérez la deuxième extrémité dans l'œillet correspondant.
DE Drücken Sie die Stangen in die Kanäle, und setzen Sie das Ende der jeweiligen Stange in die entsprechende Öse ein.

6

EN Push other end of poles until pole tip locates in the opposite grommet.
FR Disposez la deuxième extrémité de chaque arceau dans l'œillet opposé.
DE Drücken Sie die andere Ende der Stangen, bis die Stangenspitze in der gegenüberliegenden Öse sitzt.

FLY
7

EN Throw flysheet over canopy and match webbing colors at base.
FR Recouvrez la tente intérieure à l'aide du double-toit et procédez à l'assemblage en faisant correspondre les couleurs des sangles à la base.
DE Werfen Sie das Überzelt über das Innenzelt, und bringen Sie die Gurtfarben an der Bodenkante in Übereinstimmung.

8

EN Fasten Velcro® ties on underside of flysheet to pole sleeves.
FR Resserrez les attaches Velcro® situées sous le double-toit en les attachant aux fourreaux des arceaux.
DE Befestigen Sie die Klettverschlüsse, die sich an der Unterseite des Überzeltes befinden, an den Gestängekanälen.

9

EN Feed yellow pole through pole sleeve on flysheet vestibule and insert into canopy grommet.
FR Introduisez l'arceau jaune dans le fourreau de l'abside du double-toit et insérez-le dans l'œillet de la tente intérieure.
DE Schieben Sie die gelbe Stange durch den Kanal am Vorzelt (Überzelt), und setzen Sie diese in die Öse des Innenzelts ein.

10

EN Attach flysheet webbing loops over pole tips.
FR Attachez les boucles des sangles du double-toit sur les extrémités de l'arceau.
DE Verbinden Sie die Gurtschlaufen des Überzeltes mit den Stangenspitzen.

11

EN Adjust tension using ladderlocks.
FR Ajustez la tension à l'aide des dispositifs de verrouillage.
DE Regulieren Sie die Spannung mit den Abspannelementen.

12

EN Stake down the tent at all points.
FR Plantez les piquets tout autour de la tente.
DE Befestigen Sie das Zelt an allen Positionen mit Heringen.

TAKE DOWN THE TENT
EN Reverse the instructions described above. Be sure to push the poles out of their sleeves rather than pulling as the tent poles may separate when pulled. Neatly roll fly and canopy around the folded set of poles and place in stuffsack.

DÉMONTAGE DE LA TENTE
FR Reprenez les instructions ci-dessus en commençant par la fin. Assurez-vous de pousser et non pas de tirer sur les arceaux pour les retirer des fourreaux. Vous risqueriez de les séparer. Enroulez avec soin le double-toit et la tente intérieure autour des arceaux que vous aurez pliés et rangez le tout dans la housse de transport.

ABBAU DES ZELTES
DE Führen Sie die oben erläuterten Schritte in umgekehrter Reihenfolge aus. Schieben Sie die Zeltstangen aus ihren Kanälen heraus. Sie sollten die Zeltstangen aber nicht herausziehen, da sich in diesem Fall die Verbindungen der Stangen lösen. Wickeln Sie die Außenhaut und das Innenzelt sorgfältig um das Zeltstangenbündel, und verstauen Sie alles im Packsack.

COMPONENT LIST
LISTE DES ÉLÉMENTS
TEILELISTE
floor | sol | boden
3 oz/yd² nylon taffeta coated to 10,000 mm

canopy | tente intérieure | Innenzelt
1.25 oz/yd² nylon ripstop

fly | double-toit | außenhaut
2.3 oz/yd² polyester ripstop coated to 1500 mm

poles | arceaux | stangen
Seven 7001-T9 DAC Featherlite® SL shock-corded aluminum poles

stakes | piquets | heringe
Twenty-three The North Face 7075-T6 aluminum V-stakes

guylines | haubans | abspannseile
Twelve nylon guylines with reflectivity

The North Face Tent Pitching Instructions use pre-production samples for photography purposes. Material colors (including poles, webbing and fabrics) may change for production, but set-up method is accurate.

HIMALAYAN 47 SHOWN WITH FLY

HIMALAYAN 47 SHOWN WITHOUT FLY

FLY-ONLY PITCHING
EN For a lightweight, warm-weather shelter option, it is possible to pitch the flysheet independently. This is done by using the matching footprint and inserting the poles into the footprint grommets. Poles are held in place by attaching the flysheet, taking care to attach the Velcro® ties on the inside.

MONTAGE DU DOUBLE-TOIT UNIQUEMENT
FR Pour plus de légèreté lorsque les conditions climatiques le permettent, il est possible de monter séparément le double-toit. Pour cela, utilisez le tapis de sol correspondant et insérez les arceaux dans les œillets du tapis de sol. Les arceaux sont maintenus en attachant le double-toit et en prenant soin de fixer les attaches Velcro® à l'intérieur.

SEPARATES AUFSTELLEN DES AUSSENZELTES
DE Wenn bei wärmerem Wetter nur ein leichter Schutz benötigt wird, können Sie die Außenhaut separat aufstellen. Zu diesem Zweck wird die entsprechende Zeltunterlage ausgebreitet, und die Zeltstangen werden in die Ösen der Zeltunterlage eingeführt. Die Zeltstangen werden durch das Befestigen der Außenhaut und mit Hilfe von Klettverschlüssen an der Innenseite stabilisiert.

Detailed yet well-organized instructions make new product assembly less daunting.
Satellite Design

"Traditional information delivery is very linear and includes tables of contents, indexes and such. People respond to visually engaging design, but they can get easily lost if the design isn't well organized. There are benefits to the dictatorial linear structure. People need both: the comfort of someone telling them where to go next, but the attraction of multilevel visuals." —Micki Breitenstein

"'Point of view' is that quintessentially human solution to information overload, an intuitive process of reducing things to an essential relevant and manageable minimum... In a world of hyperabundant content, point of view will become the scarcest of resources." —Paul Saffo

Due to rapid company growth and product acquisition, security software leader Symantec's desktop and in-product icons began to suffer from rampant inconsistency. A new desktop and in-product icon system was created.
MetaDesign

Media sources aggregate complex data so consumers can understand and absorb the information they need.
**The *Wall Street Journal*
Information Graphics Staff**

Until fairly recently in our history, access points for information were limited. Just sixty years ago, Americans had access to a local newspaper and two or three networks on TV. Now there are hundreds of TV stations, and still, we argue, there is nothing to watch! The Internet has given us access to countless sources of news, information, products, services, online shopping experiences, social and business networking websites, email, and so much more.

More Devices Means More Interfaces.
Thanks to assorted devices (PCs, mobile phones, PDAs, MP3 players), information is coming at us 24/7 wherever we are. All the ubiquitous devices have pushed human-computer interaction design into the limelight. How we relate to the devices that deliver information is important. Someone has to think about the design of those interfaces in terms of the devices themselves (the form, shape, materials, casing, buttons, knobs, look and feel, etc.) and the design of the screens that display information on those devices.

Human-computer interaction and user interface design and engineering have been practiced since before the dawn of personal computing. There are procedures and processes in place for designing devices and interfaces. Many of these practices have infiltrated or converged with other areas of design, especially information design.

Craving the Curated Experience. With all this information flying at us, we're craving some guidance to help us sort through it. Hence the preponderance of blogs, news aggregators, content-specific RSS feeds, and an even greater need for information graphics and charts to help visually distill information. Editorial direction and thoughtful design can help us sort through and decide what's most meaningful for us. Without design and editorial oversight, all this information can feel like flat data, difficult to sort through and prioritize.

Cohesive Storytelling Online. More and more people go online to research everything from infant car seats to mortuary services. Organizations who used to have more direct contact with consumers must now rely on their online presence. They need to provide the big picture, as well as sufficient detail, to ensure consumers can find what they need.

The centralized nature of a website has driven companies to approach their organizational communications in a new way that is more cohesive than in the pre-Web days when different departments would often produce materials independently.

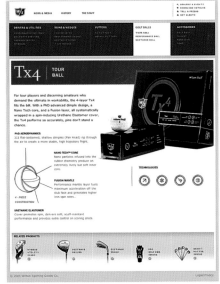

The Wilson Staff website gives consumers an easy way to access product information.
(See case study on page 184.)
VSA Partners

> **"What we need is not more information but the ability to present the right information to the right people at the right time, in the most effective and efficient form."**
>
> —Robert E. Horn

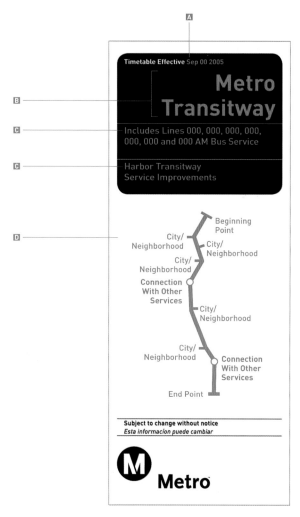

Editing the cover
Style details for editable items are listed below. For consistency across Metro timetables, character attributes should not be altered.

A Effective Date
Font: DIN Bold, 7 pt
Alignment: Left
Month: 3 characters max, title case
Day: 2 digits
Year: 4 digits

B Route No
Font: DIN Bold, 25 pt
Leading: 27 pt
Alignment: Right
Route: 2 lines max. If using only one line, use top first. If using two lines, second line should be longer than top, as shown.

C Sub-head
Font: DIN Medium, 10 pt
Leading: 11.7 pt
Alignment: Left
Text: 2 lines max

D Cover Map
Picture Box: 2.29" W x 3" H
See Cover Map section for details

← L.A. Metro had a mandate to increase ridership for the city's public transit system. The design team created detailed guidelines for streamlining transit timetables and all other rider information materials.
(See case study on page 196.)
Metro Design Studio

Complex organizations understand the value of a systematic approach to organizing their communications and telling their story. Because of this, they have turned to information architects and designers to help them with many aspects of communications beyond their online needs, including printed documents, customer service systems, internal workflow processes, and retail environments.

Rising Above the Din. In a world where there is so much information competing for attention, the smartest businesses understand that they need to differentiate their offerings. Whether they offer a product or a service, it must be more than just attractive or enticing. The experience of interacting with the product or service has to provide meaning and value. Looking great is not enough anymore. Design isn't just decoration but rather plays a critical role in creating understanding of what the business has to offer.

Companies in information-intensive fields such as financial services and health care have been among the first to understand the need to pay more attention to the way they communicate complex information to their consumers. Now, smart companies in every sector understand the need for using information design practices to differentiate themselves and gain strategic advantage.

The companies that are the most successful in the world today charge a premium because they've proved they can anticipate their customers' needs and exceed their expectations. They've thought through every detail and provide a product or service that is an elegant, seamless, and useful solution.

Replacing hundreds of post-purchase mailings with a single, personalized "owner's manual" saved Merrill Lynch $500,000 in the first 14 months of use. (See case study on page 132.)
Addison

tear drop step can
corner design: tear drop shape fits efficiently within a corner space

Packaging for simplehuman explains product benefits using simple illustrations. (See case study on page 128.)
Smart Design

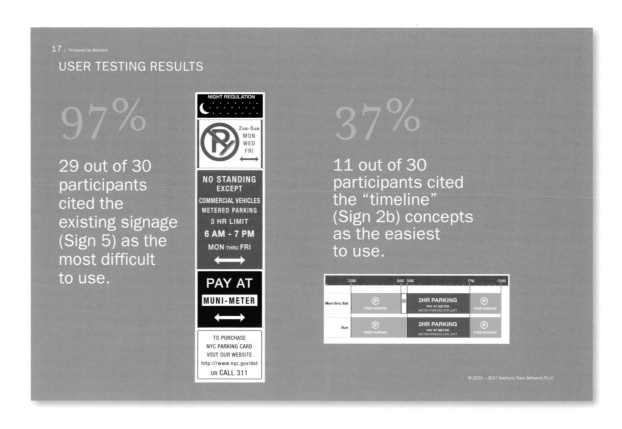

➡ This graphic compares existing New York City parking signage with an easy-to-understand timeline chart that displays parking restrictions. (See case study on page 132.)
Addison

USER TESTING RESULTS

17 / Prepared by Addison

97%

29 out of 30 participants cited the existing signage (Sign 5) as the most difficult to use.

37%

11 out of 30 participants cited the "timeline" (Sign 2b) concepts as the easiest to use.

Information Design Is Smart and Cost-efficient. The good news is that information design is cost-effective. By thoroughly thinking through all the issues of a project up front, by anticipating and respecting customer needs, and by spending time and care testing proposed solutions, information design helps organizations do it right the first time. If organizations effectively convey key messages, they can minimize the need for expensive revisions, and avoid product recalls and costly upgrades. They not only save money, they often build customer loyalty in the process.

Globalization Requires Sound Signage. For business and pleasure, more people are traveling now than ever. Large numbers of people are moving through public spaces (including travel hubs such as airports, museums, parks, city centers, and shopping malls). Multiple viewpoints and languages, and the varied levels of audience sophistication in terms of education, purpose, and travel experience, have made good information design critical for travelers trying to get from point A to point B (and multiple points beyond). Information design must be clear so that people can understand where they're going, how to get there, and what is required of them as travelers.

WHAT MAKES GOOD INFORMATION DESIGN?

Good information design is like an uneventful airline flight. There's no turbulence to remind you that you're thousands of feet in the air. You don't pause to think about the mechanics of air travel or think too hard about how such a heavy hunk of metal can be airborne. You just board, slurp your soft drink, munch on honey-roasted peanuts, and confidently arrive at your destination. When the job has been done correctly by skilled practitioners, information design can make even the most complex information quagmire look simple.

Content-focused. An information designer is like a really good translator or interpreter. To create a good piece of information design, a designer needs to understand the goal of the piece and be able to get to the essential story or set of messages. (Refer to "Wrangling Audience and Content" in Chapter 2 for details on embracing a content-oriented approach.)

User-centric. Creating designs from a user-centric mindset means that even though you're keenly aware of the client's communication goals and messaging needs for the design, you're also fully committed to understanding and catering to the needs of the end user or audience for the piece. That means learning what users actually want and need (as opposed to what you or your client think they want and need) and basing your design decisions accordingly. Having a user-centric focus means you stand up for the little guy, the user, who, without your advocacy, may not have a voice in the process.

Being user-centric also means having the awareness that there may be barriers or obstacles to understanding, and that people absorb information in different ways. For instance, some people prefer to take in visual information while others prefer auditory input. In addition, how people absorb information can be drastically influenced by diverse factors such as cultural norms, lighting, motion, and fatigue.

Finally, taking a user-centric approach to information design means that you actually ask your end users what they need out of the information design at different points in the project development process.

Tools of the Trade. A thorough understanding of the tools of the information design trade goes a long way toward ensuring solid information design output. Design principles such as hierarchy and information flow, composition and structure, weighting/grouping/rhythm of design elements, typography and type styling, use of color, use of wayfinding elements, imagery, and negative space all contribute to successful information design. (See Chapter 4, "Design Toolkit," for more details and examples.)

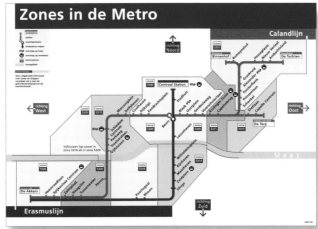

As more people travel around the globe, well-designed travel-related information graphics are more critical than ever. (See case study on page 204.)
Bureau Mijksenaar

Direct Response Design

In a cultural climate where people are overwhelmed with information at every turn, direct response advertising and marketing may be one of the tougher jobs in terms of getting people's attention. Time-challenged as we are, most people are predisposed to hating the idea of interacting with direct mail. What design strategies do direct response designers use to get people to pay attention to what might be considered junk? And what can information designers learn from their experience?

"Don't count on direct mail hanging around more than forty-eight hours. So, tell people what you want them to do. Guess what? A lot of people do it! Tell them: 'Save this catalog and refer to it,' 'Call this number now,' or 'Turn the page.'" —Kevin Kotowski

Kevin Kotowski has a long history of experience working in direct response marketing and advertising. His firm, Olson Kotowski, Inc. (OK), is an integrated, multichannel communications firm specializing in marketing, strategy, and advertising, with a focus on direct response.

At the nonprofit Natural Resources Defense Council (NRDC), Liz Linke is the print/art director and Linda Lopez is head of membership. The NRDC's direct mail efforts are focused on fundraising and awareness rather than on selling a product or service, but the direct marketing goals are similar.

Have you noticed any recent trends in direct mail?

OK: In the last several years there have been changes in direct mail. You used to hear the saying, "Neatness is the enemy of involvement." A lot of direct mail packages would have devices for involvement (stamps you might place on the reply card, rub-offs, quizzes, etc.) scattered throughout. We don't see that much anymore. People are time-challenged and they're much more marketing and design savvy.

What do you need to do to create effective direct mail pieces these days?

OK: The information has to be organized, with headers that are scannable, so people can get the information quickly. If they want to read more in-depth, they can. Typography has become more important. Reverse type tends to squash readability and comprehension.

NRDC: Test and steal. To see what works and what doesn't in direct mail, get yourself on every list. See what packages organizations and companies are sending through the mail. If they keep mailing the same package, that means it's working for them. Try to figure out why that design works for them.

Explain how testing for direct mail works.

NRDC: Traditional marketing firms do focus groups and polling. With direct mail, we test by sending it out. If the package brings us money, then we know it's working. You send out a small sample, then you send the package to more people.

What else works and what doesn't in terms of design for direct response?

OK: We've found the following techniques can be effective:

- Neatness, organization, and getting to the point quickly makes a difference.

- Put photo captions right under the image so people know exactly what they're looking at.

- Surrounding a product with callouts helps people absorb information quickly.

- Make sure the toll-free phone number and web URL info are easy to find.

- The business reply card still works really well for lead generation. People often look at the reply card before they look at everything else. Putting more than one reply card in the piece works well.

- The coolest advertising doesn't always win. If it doesn't communicate and get someone to act, it's not working.

NRDC: Through testing, we've found that:

- Celebrity names help people notice the package, as long as there's a good match between the issue and the celebrity.

- Photos don't seem to work. We've tested them.

- Because we're a nonprofit, the fewer design elements there are, and the simpler the piece is, the more credible people find it.

- Communicate urgency (as long as it's credible and not false urgency).

- Red and black are the colors that get people's attention and signify action and urgency.

- To fight list fatigue, change the package slightly (example: reverse everything out to black), and you'll get a bump in response because people don't realize that they've seen the piece already.

- Getting someone to open the envelope is the most important thing you can do in direct mail marketing. It's more important than what you have inside.

What about the shelf life of direct response pieces?

OK: Don't count on direct mail hanging around more than forty-eight hours. So, tell people what you want them to do. Guess what? A lot of people do it! Tell them: "Save this catalog and refer to it," "Call this number now," or "Turn the page."

How important is the copywriting?

OK: Copy/content is where direct mail started. For a while, there was a de-emphasis on copy. We're seeing it swing back because with the web, marketers realized that content was king. Not enough relevant content means you fail.

NRDC: Copywriting is more important than the design of the package in our case. The message is key and everything boils down to credibility.

OK: The test we use: Can they really understand what we're trying to tell them without reading all of the body copy from beginning to end? If they can do that, we'll probably have a successful piece.

What about the expense of sending out mailings?

OK: Postal regulations and rate increases come along every couple of years and it costs more to put stuff in the mail. New postal rates haven't made an impact on what companies are willing to do. Clients are willing to test something oversized or dimensional or different—something that stands out. It may cost more to mail, but if you get greater response, it's often worth it to break through the clutter.

NRDC: Even though it is more expensive to mail out a larger sized package like a 9 x 12-inch (22.9 x 30.5 cm) envelope, we tend to get better response with larger formats.

Are companies and organizations using more or less direct response in their marketing plans?

OK: Companies are using direct mail and direct response communications now more than ever because CEOs are demanding accountable, measurable results.

NRDC: People have been saying that direct mail is dead for decades, but it still lives.

Litigation Graphics

In the legal profession, where the stakes are often quite high, clear communication is paramount. Judges and juries find themselves making weighty decisions about scientific and technical matters that are completely unfamiliar to them, so the niche field of courtroom and litigation information graphics is becoming a key component of the litigation process. We spoke with two litigation graphics experts about the ways in which good information design supports litigation. Airan Wright is a designer and consultant at Zagnoli McEvoy Foley LLC (ZMF), a Chicago-based firm specializing in litigation communication and consulting, including litigation graphics. Jeff Isler is the principal and senior consultant for InfoGraphics, a New York–based trial support firm that focuses on litigation support, including litigation graphics.

"In the courtroom, we're trying to teach. What sets litigation apart from other endeavors is that we're teaching and arguing. You have highly trained professionals with lots at stake. Somebody wins and somebody loses." —Jeff Isler

Who typically hires you?

AW: ZMF is typically hired by lawyers interested in getting help with developing their case themes both orally and visually.

JI: We're hired by lawyers and occasionally by a corporation. Ideally, it's a close working relationship between lawyers and the graphic design team. We help refine and convert their information in visual terms, but the argument and the underlying strategy is theirs.

What makes doing litigation graphics unique as a field?

JI: In the courtroom, we're trying to teach. What sets litigation apart from other endeavors is that we're teaching and arguing. You have highly trained professionals with lots at stake. Somebody wins and somebody loses.

AW: A designer has to understand the case before starting work. Design in litigation focuses on function first. A graphic has to be able to tell its story clearly and concisely in a few seconds. One of the most interesting aspects of this field is that you get to become a mini-expert in a lot of different fields.

What is the process for creating litigation graphics?

JI: The process varies from client to client. Typically, we get a call and the lawyer gives us a bare-bones explanation of the case, so that we can do a conflict check to make sure we're not doing work for the other side. We provide consulting, design, and technology. Often, we need information from experts. For legal reasons, all discussions happen with an attorney present.

AW: First, the team meets with the lead attorneys and experts. Once we understand the case and all the key points that we need to show, I look for the best way to show them graphically. That could be using animation, a physical model/prototype, a video, a presentation board, an interactive Flash piece, or a PowerPoint presentation.

What is the revision process like for litigation graphics?

AW: We agree to do a set number of revisions to a graphic, but we almost never stick to that. We iterate and make as many changes as needed. I've been in situations where we're in the courtroom changing graphics minutes before they're used.

JI: Having enough time is one of our greatest challenges. We've created certain proprietary solutions around the concept of having to make changes quickly at the last minute. The graphic is essentially designed to be changed.

How often does your work see the light of the courtroom?

JI: Most cases settle, but we prepare as if we will go to trial.

AW: The vast majority of our graphics are never seen by a jury. Despite that, having finished graphics available at all stages of the game shows that a lawyer is prepared to argue his or her point.

What design and communications tools work best to help tell the story in terms of litigation graphics?

JI: What you are preparing for is a performance. The best litigators begin early in the development process to plan their presentation as a performance that will happen in front of a judge and jury. To help them, I must think the same way. I imagine that performance from both the attorney's point of view and from the jury's. As a juror, what would make me skeptical about the material? What arguments would I accept? It's nuancing and gamesmanship. People learn through stories. I call it narrative design. Some attorneys are brilliant in their ability to string together their narratives on the fly. For them, I build modular components that they can mix, match, and reorder on the fly. Most attorneys do better if we provide them with the narrative designed right into the presentation.

AW: Each point you wish to make must be presented clearly. Choosing the right medium makes a big difference. Sometimes a large 4 x 6-foot (1.2 x 1.8 m) trial board is better than a PowerPoint presentation because a board can sit out in front of the audience for hours, illustrating the key points a legal team wants to hammer home. Other times, an animation might work better. Once, a coworker of mine had a car cut into quarters and brought into the courtroom because that was the best way to illustrate the point.

JI: We always have to clarify with the attorney: What is the exact conclusion the viewer should take away from seeing this graphic? Because we're going into a courtroom, the more overtly designed anything is, the more manipulated a jury often feels. Animation is a wonderful tool and we use it all the time. But I make sure my clients understand that when I create a 3-D animation it's completely fabricated. It's informational, enjoyable, and compelling. But if you're going to be slick, it's got to be a conscious choice.

Are there any dos and don'ts specific to litigation graphics?

JI: The attorney shouldn't be explaining the graphics. The graphics are supposed to support the words! If not, I've failed.

AW: In litigation graphics, you have less leeway in terms of design than with other design fields. We do have some unofficial rules. Pantone 1235 Coated reads as a really nice yellow on a projected screen. Red means bad or stop. Avoid red and green together because many people relate that color combination to Christmas. The simplest approach is best. You need to be considerate of your jurors' situation and help them learn in the clearest and simplest manner.

Civic Policy and Information Design

Decisions are made every day that impact the way millions of people live, work, and interact in community environments. Information design is beginning to play a key role in helping city officials and citizens simplify and communicate complex matters so that they can move forward with insight, intelligence, and a clear grasp of the issues. Application of information design principles and creation of helpful documentation can lead to surprising and inspiring results.

PHILADELPHIA—FIGHT OR FLIGHT?

The Problem: Dry, Bland Reports. The Metropolitan Philadelphia Policy Center needed a regional report on the five-county region to cover a wide range of issues such as urban flight, suburban sprawl, employment, education, and taxation. Such reports are written to educate and inform corporate leaders, policy-makers, and others striving to make a difference in the region. Reports of this nature are often long-winded, dry, negative in tone, and rarely designed to be accessible for readers.

No One Said Reports Have to Be Inaccessible. The Baltimore, Maryland, firm Rutka Weadock Design reinterpreted the nature of the weighty government report. The result was evocatively titled "Fight or Flight." The firm's principals explain: "We wanted the piece to look authoritative but still be compelling to a wide audience. We decided to design a piece that looked more like a book and less like a brochure."

The book is perfect-bound and sized at 6.5 x 9.25 inches (16.1 x 23.5 cm), a distinctive format compared to the usual report. To set an inviting tone, the book's full-color, thirty-two-page introductory section includes positive messages about the Philadelphia region. The rest of the book's eighty pages provide deeper access to information but still feature color to highlight and draw attention. A number of simply designed charts and maps make key data highly accessible.

Wake-up Call. The firm says, "It worked; the response has been tremendous." That response has included levels of community involvement that haven't been seen in Philadelphia since the 1960s and 1970s. Citizens and business leaders came out in droves for a rally to fight the wage tax, citing the Fight or Flight report as an inspiration. Apparently, quite a few gubernatorial candidates for Pennsylvania were seen carrying dog-eared copies of the book. Says the project's main client contact, Karen L. Black, director of the Metropolitan Philadelphia Policy Center, "It is clear that we did what we set out to do; we educated regional leadership about the state of the region and mobilized them to act—to make the effort to bring positive change to Metropolitan Philadelphia. We have clearly woken up people in this region."

TRAFFIC CONFUSION AND SOLUTION

The City of South Pasadena, California, was in the process of developing a plan to solve local traffic congestion problems. The city council labored for over a year to identify and choose among various traffic congestion-management project options.

"They decided to hold a public forum to gain wider community feedback," explains Gay Forbes, former assistant city manager of the City of South Pasadena. "However, engineering drawings were much too detailed to be useful to the general public, and were very confusing."

Graphics Clarified the Situation. Design firm KBDA was hired to assist the engineers in explaining the impact of the proposed improvements. The KBDA team, which included an information architect and a graphic designer, worked closely with the engineering and landscape architecture teams to clarify and simplify the data, and to create a series of diagrams demonstrating the impact of the different plans on traffic, parking, sidewalks, and landscaping, as well as the impact on local businesses and residences.

The diagrams allowed the highly technical, detail-oriented engineering team to communicate complex information with a great deal of simplicity. The engineers presented the diagrams at a public forum. The community was able to understand each of the plans and approve a course of action for the street improvement project.

DETROIT'S CIVIC MAPS—THERAPY FOR A CITY'S SELF-IMAGE

City with a Past. Detroit is a region seeking to move beyond racial tension and ongoing economic challenges.

These issues have resulted in a city that is generally poor, minority-populated, and underserved, surrounded by some of the most affluent suburbs in the nation. Motivated by narrow, sometimes parochial interests, many in the region have worked to distance themselves from each other instead of forging a shared sense of destiny.

Balkanization vs. a Centralized Viewpoint. The Detroit Metro Convention and Visitors Bureau engaged California-based Applied Storytelling to revitalize its tourism brand and present a cohesive picture of metro Detroit. The project outcome, a series of Destination District Maps, serves as an aid to visitors, but also a tool for residents of Detroit's diverse communities. The immediate goal: increased tourism. The potential lasting effect: a new sense of shared identity and purpose for Detroit residents and businesses.

Eric La Brecque of Applied Storytelling explains, "You can't attach value to something until you understand what it means to you. Detroit has been undervalued by tourists, but also by residents. The city has been Balkanized. In previous maps, you see dozens of borders and boundaries. We needed a more compelling and cohesive story. That story is manifested through new maps, which don't create an 'us vs. you' perception of the region."

Rebranding a City with Maps. "In surveys and focus groups," explains Jim Townsend, director of Detroit's Tourism Economic Development Council, "visitors told us that they struggled to find the 'good stuff' in metro Detroit." In response, five "Tourism Destination Districts" were identified. The maps offer a simple graphical tool for identifying concentrations of interesting things for people to do in each newly defined district.

Maps Made Accessible. Says La Brecque, "The Destination Maps are a mental scheme rather than a precise mapping. We cited the London Underground map as one inspiration. Why not apply this same thinking to the way you envision a city above ground? From a cognitive standpoint, the maps deliver only what's meaningful. Information becomes practical and digestible."

Adoption and Change in Perception. How can a city adopt a new way of thinking of itself? Information design has helped. "Maps can be hugely sticky," says La Brecque. "The Destination District Maps show the key areas of Detroit organized in a way that makes sense geographically, but also conceptually. The maps help people see that neighborhoods aren't so far apart. There aren't as many actual boundaries as people imagined. There's a diminished sense of 'otherness.' People in Detroit see the maps and are happy and relieved. It's like someone has opened their eyes to a relationship they had been uncomfortable acknowledging for the past forty years."

This unusual government report, designed to be both captivating and informative, proved to be a useful tool for a number of Philadelphia constituents.
Rutka Weadock Design

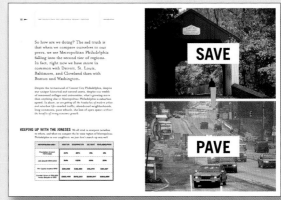

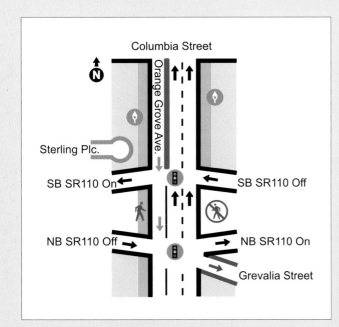

Columbia Street

Orange Grove Ave.

Sterling Plc.

SB SR110 On   SB SR110 Off

NB SR110 Off   NB SR110 On

Grevalia Street

This information graphic helped the City of South Pasadena choose and approve a street improvement plan.
KBDA

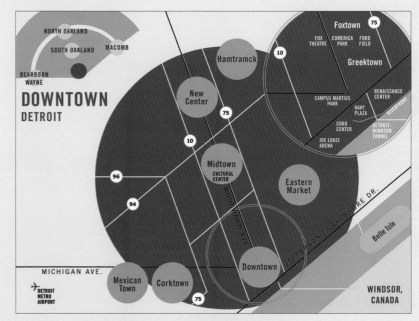

Detroit was originally built on a radial plan. The new maps take direct visual cues from the radial concept. Jim Townsend, director of Detroit's Tourism Economic Development Council, notes, "How wonderful from a wayfinding standpoint to have a compass imprinted onto the city and its surrounding region!"
Applied Storytelling

Designers routinely face design projects that are more and more complex. In particular, information design projects require careful thought, collaboration, planning, and a process that goes beyond the intuitive, gut-level, and sometimes solitary approach that many designers have been trained to use.

PROCESS: DISCOVERY

2

→ Politics, Diplomacy, and Consensus

→ Wrangling Audience and Content

→ The Creative Brief

→ Personas and Scenarios

Politics, Diplomacy, and Consensus

> "We regarded it as unacceptable to say that a design might have worked but for the politics. Given the major role that political, social, and economic issues played in the outcome of design projects, we thought it important to develop methodologies that took account of these issues." —David Sless

WHAT MAKES YOUR CLIENT TICK?

Many factors that determine the success of a design piece are unrelated to the formal aspects of design but have everything to do with the context in which the design is created.

More and more information designers find that to create relevant solutions for their clients, they need to find out about the inner workings of the organization, its politics, its goals, and agendas. Why is that? First, by finding out what makes an organization tick, you'll be able to offer smarter solutions. Second, by understanding the inner workings of an organization, you'll be able to create the kind of teamwork, collaboration, and consensus with your client that you need to achieve project success.

INTERNAL BUSINESS STRUCTURES

Understanding your client's business structure has enormous value, especially when there's a complex business hierarchy in place. What departments will participate in the project? What will their involvement be? Who has a stake in the outcome?

Client History 101. Have similar projects been undertaken within the organization before? Who participated and will they be involved in this project? Was the experience positive or negative overall? What were the roadblocks or challenges? How did they measure success? Learning a little bit of background about what happened prior to your arrival can be quite illuminating and useful. Understanding your client's internal challenges and decision-making methods allows you to be proactive in terms of both your process and the design solutions you ultimately present.

Cultivate Allies. Who among your client team understands the project process already, and who can be educated about the process to the point where they will be your best advocates? It helps to make sure you cultivate allies both at the

A microsite design project for Nike Investor Relations needed to fit into the overall business hierarchy and Web organization structure of Nike.com. This diagram was created to help the diverse client teams understand the navigational challenges. **KBDA**

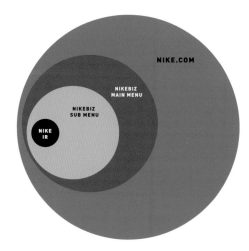

NIKE.COM

NIKEBIZ
MAIN MENU

NIKEBIZ
SUB MENU

NIKE
IR

grassroots level of the organization and at the higher decision-making levels. Obviously, having great rapport and understanding with people at the highest decision-making levels will aid you greatly in obtaining buy-in for your designs. Developing solid relationships with the grassroots people in the organization can give you additional insight into the client's internal machinations and can help you grease the project's wheels.

Who Wields the Power? The person who is the ultimate decision-maker should be at the table for the kickoff meeting. This is critical. If the person with veto power isn't present, you could spend weeks or even months creating a design solution that has no chance of being approved because, for example, the ultimate decision-maker hates the color green. Be sure to ask at the outset: Is there anyone else who could swoop in and change the rules or nature of the project? Is there any other circumstance or internal client agenda that could impact the project?

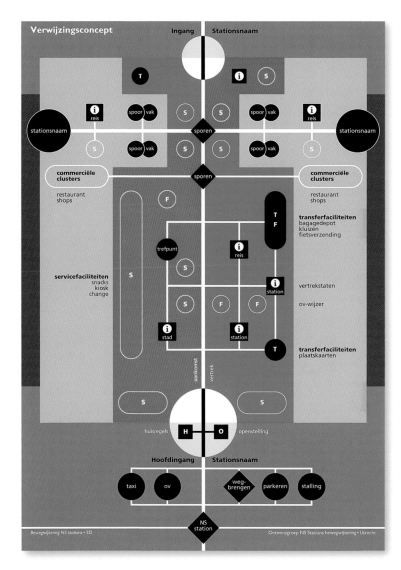

Sometimes design projects require balancing the needs of different constituencies. For example, in planning a wayfinding system for a public transit hub such as an airport, commercial interests are balanced with travelers' needs. (See case study on page 204.) **Bureau Mijksenaar**

"What Americans call politics, Europeans call bureaucracy. Ultimately it comes down to competing departments defending their own turf. Politics sounds as if it's untouchable, as if you can't do anything about it. But you can create change." —Paul Mijksenaar

OUTLINE THE PROCESS, TEAM, AND ROLES

Diagram the Process. Even before project work begins, explain and outline the process so that everyone involved gets the big picture. Make sure everyone working on the project, including your design team and the client team, understands their roles and responsibilities. Document the steps in the process so that team members can refer to it down the line.

Who's on the Team? Make a list of everyone's roles, responsibilities, and contact information, including email, snail mail address (in case you have to ship something overnight), fax numbers, and office and cell phone numbers. You can't always assume that the project manager has all the info. There may be an emergency where the PM isn't available. Of course, you'll want to set up contact protocols. Most of the back-and-forth contact will happen between the two project managers (one on the design side and one on the client side). And while it's true that you may not want the junior designer to randomly phone the client's CEO just for the heck of it, you do want to make sure that any critical contact info is handy for the team in case of an urgent situation.

Assign Point People. Who will be the day-to-day point person on your team and on the client team? You'll need to make sure you've got people on both sides of the project to guide it throughout all stages.

This work plan diagram breaks down a project week by week to help the team plan ahead.
Matter

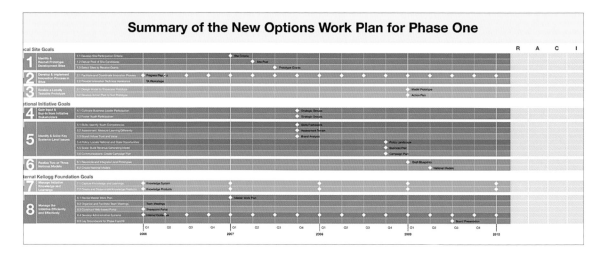

"Politics is about people's interests. People argue for and define what is of interest to them materially and organizationally. People's eyes will often roll at this unpleasant stuff called politics, but the reality is that it's ever-present and will up and bite you." —David Sless

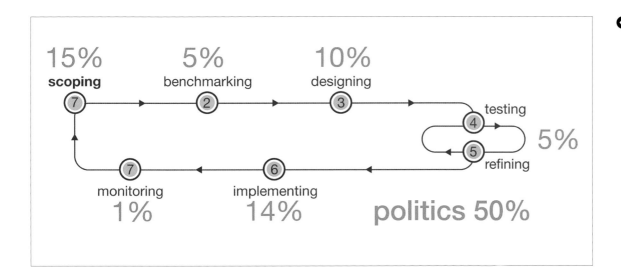

The Communication Research Institute in Australia points out that an inordinate amount of time in every information design project is spent in meetings, and on tasks related to process and project management. For a long time, the organization hadn't been able to charge for this time. Now the method they use to budget for projects is simple: They go through all the technical and design specifications, figure the time that will be required, and then double it. **Communication Research Institute, Australia**

The Timeline. Before you create the project timeline, find out about client expectations and make sure they are realistic. Determine which of the drivers for the timeline are truly fixed, and which can't be changed. (For instance, the client is going on national television and the website needs to be up and running in plenty of time.)

Of course, every client wants the project done yesterday, if not sooner. Most projects have a sense of urgency, which is a good thing. A healthy sense of urgency ensures that everyone takes the job seriously, and

this means the work will get done in a timely manner to the benefit of the team, client, and end users. But try to see if you can separate the truly important deadline situations from false urgency. You want to set up the project in a way that will give you the best work within a reasonable timeline. Sometimes clients impress upon you a false sense of urgency and you rush to completion. You may not have quite enough time to do what you really want to do and may be forced into cutting corners only to find out that the deadline was based on something relatively inconsequential.

Conclusion: The Water's Fine. While it's true that you can just dive into the project head-first and figure things out as you go along, we don't recommend that approach. A little bit of planning and setup, a clearly defined team, some knowledge about the client—all of these things can really help the process so there are fewer surprises and pitfalls once you get down to the business of designing.

Wrangling Audience and Content

KNOW THY AUDIENCE

A huge part of the planning process for an intelligently planned information design piece centers on the audience. Before you strategize with your client about what the piece says, the team first has to learn more about audience needs and goals, and about how audience goals align with a client's business strategy.

Identify and Prioritize. It's critical to identify all the possible audiences for the piece you're about to design. Why is each audience type vital to the client? Which members of the audience are most important? Many clients will emphatically insist: They're all equally important! But at the end of the day there is usually a short list of audience members who take precedence. Help your client identify who is on the short list and then prioritize them. As you move forward with the design of the piece, you may run into situations where audience needs are in conflict. Informed decisions can be made based on who is at the top of the heap in terms of priority.

UNDERSTAND THE REQUIREMENTS

What does the audience need to know and why do they need to know it?

Emotional Requirements. How do you want your audience to respond emotionally to the information? Do you want to reassure them? Inspire them? Motivate them to do something?

Physical Requirements. It's critical to anticipate the physical context in which information will be reviewed.

- Are they going to be interacting with the designed piece while they're walking, working, or in repose?

- Does this audience like to read?

- Will they be reading the piece in one sitting, or over time?

- Is the piece meant to be read only once, or will the audience need to refer to it repeatedly?

- Will the piece be designed and presented in a single language, and if so, will the audience be fluent in that language? Will the piece need to be translated?

- Will an older demographic and poor eyesight be a factor?

- Will the tendency for readers to want to avoid dense material need to be accommodated?

(See "Personas and Scenarios," page 58, for more information on how to map out useful details about audience needs and requirements.)

"Insight is what is created as we add context and give care to both the presentation and organization of data, as well as the particular needs of our audience." —Nathan Shedroff

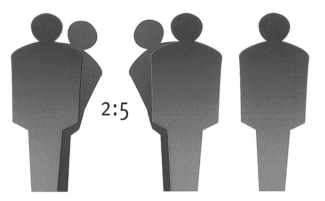

2:5

Chances that an American is shy:

How can information design address emotional aspects of information? This graphic depicts the percentage of Americans who claim they suffer from shyness.
Sonia Chia

7th St/Metro Center Connections

1.800.COMMUTE
metro.net

M Metro

L.A. Metro's connections map orients customers as they exit a train, helping them reach their ultimate destination. The map lists connecting services in addition to important surface street landmarks, so travelers can see where they are and where they're headed. (See case study on page 196.)
Metro Design Studio

Organizing Content: The Alphanumeric Solution

Information-dense projects such as books or websites can contain heaps of content. In cases where a large amount of content needs to be developed, there are often multiple producers or writers. The process of organizing different pieces of content from various sources can be a bit like herding cats, and can take its toll on the project budget, not to mention team members' sanity.

Here's a simple but effective "best practice" you and your clients might consider using to create and maintain order throughout the life of a project. It shows how—using a simple alphanumeric device—content was organized for a text-heavy website, from project inception through the site launch. The point is not to create complexity for the mere sake of it, but to create a simple tool that can be used across project phases.

This full sitemap for the KBDA project for the Prostate Cancer Foundation (PCF) shows the alphanumeric system when it was first put into place for the project.

1 Devise a numbering system and use it to organize and label content from day one. The following examples show an effective model, but feel free to experiment. The system just needs to be simple to use and work for the team.

2 Apply your numbering system to documentation early in the process. For example, early-stage documents for most websites include the sitemap and wireframes. Each section of the sitemap chart is assigned a letter and its subsections follow a predetermined numeric code. The wireframe pages should also be numbered according to the system. Again, the alphanumeric system is a simple device, but helps the team stay focused on what they're looking at as the project documentation evolves.

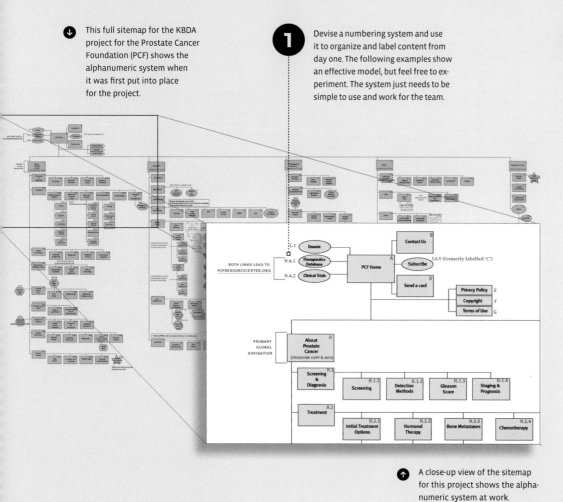

A close-up view of the sitemap for this project shows the alphanumeric system at work.

The file name for this MS Word file and the document header include the numbering system.

A SYSTEM YOU CAN LOVE

An alphanumeric system is a simple way to effectively communicate with the team about assorted pieces of content over the long course of a complicated project.

The system becomes a kind of shorthand method for the team. The project manager, looking for a particular piece of content from the client, can ask, "Do you have the content for page H.2.3, Bone Metastases?" The client might reply, "Yes, we are just finishing up H.2.3, but we changed the title."

Things like nomenclature changes or changes in content order are much easier to track and are much less confusing with the numbering system in place. When you can plug each piece of content into the system, it's also much easier to track which pieces have been delivered and what's still missing from your content deck. By setting up and using a simple system like the one outlined here, you can eliminate a lot of pain and suffering from the content wrangling process.

3 Continue to apply the numbering system to other documents as they are produced throughout the project. Update the system as necessary when content is reorganized, added, or deleted from the project. For example, if the order of pages on the site changes, the numbering system is revised so the hierarchy is accurately documented and the numbering system can be used as a reference point during project discussions.

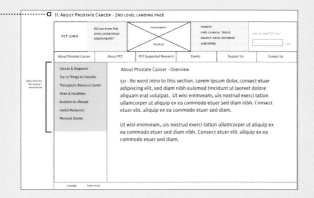

↑ This wireframe image shows the layout for site section H., About Prostate Cancer. Notice how the wireframe page header uses the numbering system set up on the sitemap.

↑ The design layout file itself should also be labeled with the alphanumeric system. This way, everyone understands which part of the project is being mocked up, and can refer to the previous documentation if there are questions or discussion points.

→ File folders for the digital assets of the project can also be organized according to the numbering system. Notice how the file folders themselves mirror the system on the sitemap. The MS Word document file name is also labeled according to the system.

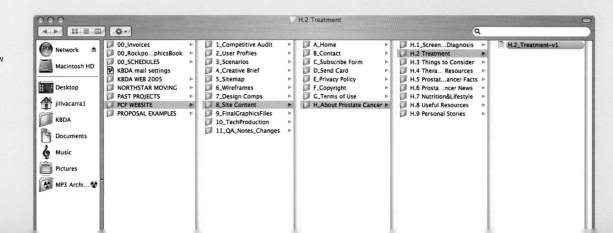

Pull quotes, captions, and timeline graphics were introduced into this annual report to provide multiple entry points to readers and to ensure that key messages surfaced.
KBDA

improvements in hemoglobin and other measures than patients treated with EPO alone or EPO plus oral iron. These improvements are an important benefit to patients undergoing cancer treatment.

In early 2002, we began Phase II feasibility trials to evaluate Ferrlecit® in the treatment of anemia in cancer patients receiving supplemental EPO therapy. We believe that our product can address this serious medical need and improve the quality of life for these patients.

In addition to our efforts in the treatment of cancer-associated anemia, we are considering other iron deficiency anemia applications, such as chronic kidney disease and iron deficiencies associated with acute blood loss in surgical procedures. Together, these potential new applications could represent significant market expansion opportunities for Ferrlecit®. As we gather additional data, we intend to formulate strategies for supporting new avenues of growth that provide solutions to similarly unanswered needs.

Better delivery methods

We also expand our portfolio by improving the ways that medications are delivered, thereby improving the patient's quality of life through better therapy.

Today, our products utilize a wide spectrum of delivery methods, including oral, topical, transdermal and transmucosal delivery. We strive to develop the delivery method that yields the greatest benefit with the lowest possible side effects. A perfect example is another Watson-developed branded product that will receive a major development push in 2002: our antifungal, onychomycosis topical patch.

Exactly how many people in the United States are affected by nail fungal infections is difficult to judge. Estimates are that 15% to 20% of adults between 40 and 60 years of age are affected, with 10 million to 12 million Americans currently diagnosed. Despite

We also expand our portfolio by improving the ways that medications are delivered. We strive to develop the delivery method that yields the greatest benefit with the lowest possible side effects.

Gain insight into what may be less obvious. In this way, you can create a path others may overlook.

1996
Watson enters the branded arena with one branded product and a sales force of four.

2001
Watson has over 30 branded product lines, with more than $555 million in 2001 branded product revenues, and a branded sales force exceeding 400.

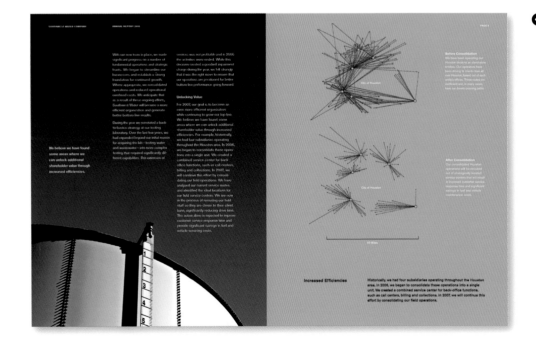

Frequent subheads, short text line lengths, and captioned before-and-after graphics made this annual report easy to scan for information.
KBDA

Chunks of information grouped by color in short paragraphs helped make this invitation for a large London culinary event easy and fun to read.
thomas.matthews

CONTENT CAN BE A MOVING TARGET

The business world has changed dramatically over the last decade. Companies must constantly redefine their markets and business models, while seeking higher rates of productivity. They must often accomplish these Herculean tasks with fewer internal resources and a leaner workforce. Long ago, clients approached designers with final content ready to be produced. In a business environment that is constantly evolving, today's clients are often hard-pressed to find the time and clarity to think through their communications issues, much less develop refined, on-target content.

Guide the Content Creation Design. It's safe to say that information design combines communication and content more directly and thoroughly than almost any other design discipline. Design and content processes continually inform each other.

Today's information designer may be faced with the unexpected challenge of having to help the client think through the content at several stages of the project.

There are times when a client will deliver content and you'll discover real challenges with the writing tone or the message. Other times the copy may only need simple refinements.

Information Design as Advocacy. Even the most organized clients may need your help, or at the very least your "bird's-eye view." In addition to thinking through the design issues, you can be a key advocate for the end user. If you have a difficult time immediately grasping the content, chances are the reader will have a hard time too—especially since a typical reader will quickly turn away from information that is difficult to absorb. You'll be most valuable to clients when you are simultaneously "half in" and "half out" of their organization so that you can offer informed, objective advice.

Plain Language

The written word is a key component of information design. There is a movement afoot toward ensuring that written information is clear, concise, and meaningful for readers. It's called plain language. We spoke with William Lutz, the plain language advocate and expert practitioner who, among other things, wrote _A Plain English Handbook: How to Create Clear SEC Disclosure Documents_, which offered clear guidelines from the U.S. Securities and Exchange Commission on writing investor information.

What is plain language's connection to good information design?

WL: Plain language uses words economically and at a level the audience can understand. Its sentence structure is tight. Its tone is welcoming and direct. Its design is visually appealing. A plain language document is easy to read and looks like it's meant to be read.

How do you convey complex information with plain language?

WL: It's not "Dick and Jane" and "See Spot run." Plain language does not mean you delete complex information to make the document easier to understand. Sometimes documents must impart complex information. Using plain language assures the orderly and clear presentation of complex information so that readers have the best possible chance of understanding it.

What are some other misconceptions about implementing plain language?

WL: One concern I hear often is that if a document is written clearly and in plain language, then people won't take it seriously.

I run into this all the time with lawyers. A bank was worried that they wouldn't be taken seriously if their materials were in plain language. You can write clearly but in a serious tone.

What are the roots of the plain language movement? Where is it being practiced?

WL: Well, you can say it goes back to England in the sixteenth century when one particular lawyer produced an unbelievably long document for the court. The Chancellor had a hole cut in the document and had the guy wear it as a collar. People have always struggled with issues of clear communication. In our age of communication, with the growth of mass communication, we become even more aware of the need for clarity in language. Some other countries are way ahead of us in terms of adopting plain language. Some Scandinavian countries have a degree program; you can't offer plain language services unless you're certified. The South African constitution is written in plain language. The French government, sick and tired of too many complicated forms, has also initiated a plain language movement. Great Britain is in the process of rewriting all its tax laws and regulations into plain language.

What are some examples of tangible plain language benefits?

WL: There's plenty of documentation on the real cost savings of plain language. In business, it's a bottom-line issue. When Merrill Lynch instituted their plain language program, they immediately noted a cost savings of $500,000 (£239,327). When the British postal system redesigned a single form—the equivalent of our change of address form—the rate of incorrectly completed forms dropped significantly, and they estimated a savings of about $1.5 million in U.S. dollars (£717,983).

Do you have any cautionary tales where plain language would have made a huge difference?

WL: One of my favorite examples is from the Three Mile Island disaster. The memo that was sent to the engineering operations staff right before the accident was supposed to alert staff to the possibility of a malfunction at the plant, but was so confusingly written that it failed to communicate the situation properly. That badly written memo resulted in about $3 billion (£1,439,700,000) in clean-up expenses.

How is the process different for writing plain language?

WL: SEC Chairman Arthur Levitt said, "Plain language calls for a new way of thinking." Writing plain language is not about reformatting and making shorter sentences. You have to rethink the whole document. What is it you want to say, who are you saying it to, for what reason?

What's different in writing plain language for online content?

WL: For online documents, you have to think three-dimensionally. You need to plan for users to click through to more information. When designing, always make sure the person can print out everything—including the dropdown menus.

Do you have any other basic tips for creating documents and information design that communicate well?

WL: Page design should clearly inform the reader as to where they are in the text. Type hierarchy is something that information designers use for clarity. It's amazing how many long documents you find without running heads or subheads. That's an issue of accessibility. Make sure you include simple things like a table of contents.

If I'm an information designer looking to collaborate with a plain language expert, where do I find one?

WL: Look online for a plain language expert. There are companies that specialize. Be careful, because some companies who say they do it have a very different idea of plain language. Look at before-and-after examples of their work to be sure.

What about companies and organizations with a different agenda? Aren't there some who don't want to communicate clearly, who want to confuse on purpose?

WL: Of course. But as more and more companies use plain language and information design, clear communication will become more of a standard. People will get used to it. If an organization doesn't communicate clearly, there will be the presumption that they're hiding something.

"Writing plain language is not about reformatting and making shorter sentences. You have to rethink the whole document. What is it you want to say, who are you saying it to, for what reason?" —William Lutz

Spec the job

A typical 10K printed on Mohawk Options Smooth, 100% PCW Cream White 70 text (101,000 sheets or 14,140 pounds); 100,000 copies; 1c/1c, saddle stitch booklet, finished size 8.5 x 11, generates environmental benefits equivalent to:

Not driving 7070 miles in an average automobile

12567 lbs. net greenhouse gases prevented

96,152,000 BTUs of energy not consumed

6830 lbs. of solid waste not generated

135.74 preserved for the future

57,661 gallons wastewater flow saved

391.97 lbs. of waterborne waste not generated

Source: Mohawk Environmental Calculator available at www.Mohawkpaper.com. Conversions are provided by the EDF (Environmental Defense Fund) and/or the U.S. EPA.

The design team for this Mohawk brochure project was involved at the beginning of the process to help define the content approach. This ensured a perfect integration of writing and design. (See case study on page 140.)
And Partners

CONTENT ANALYSIS

There Could Be Gold in Those Mountains of Data. Whenever we start a new project, we like to hear the beep-beep-beeping sound of a large dump truck backing up to our office to unload mountains of data and documentation. The more you know about a client's history, their business sector, and past projects, the better you can solve the design problem at hand.

- Ask the client for access to any related strategic plans, or information on tangential initiatives, that may impact your project directly or indirectly. The idea is to align your design approach with the client's long-term goals.

- Often, clients have existing market research, which you can leverage to better inform the project team and process.

- Review and analyze previous versions of the project, if available.

- Review other previously produced client materials. Your project, once complete, will likely be seen in conjunction with these other materials.

- Consider auditing relevant competitor materials and building a competitor matrix that compares and contrasts your client's competitors.

- With client input, locate "best of breed" examples of similar kinds of projects and discuss these with the project team.

Content Strategy: See the Forest and the Trees. As you assist your client in thinking through the strategic development of content, we recommend you address the following:

- Are the project goals clear and well thought out?

- What does the project need to achieve? (This usually includes multiple goals: for the audiences, for the client, and possibly for other constituents.)

- Define success. If the project is wildly successful, what results will be gained?

- Identify any assumptions that have been made about the audiences, the need for the project, and the specific deliverables. For example, while KBDA was developing a new website design for the UCLA Anderson School of Management, the client team felt certain that the content should be targeted toward faculty users. However, post-launch site-traffic data confirmed what we originally suspected: The majority of site visitors are still prospective students. Consequently, KBDA continues to work with the school to adjust the site design to reflect a more student-focused sensibility.

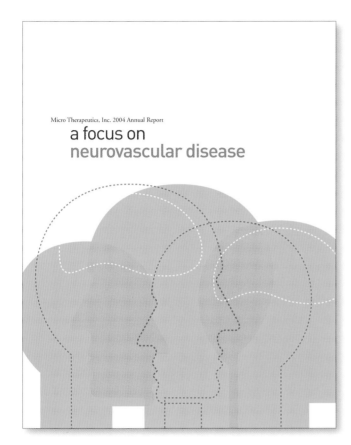

Micro Therapeutics, Inc. 2004 Annual Report

a focus on
neurovascular disease

Micro Therapeutics, Inc. developed products for the treatment of neurovascular disorders associated with stroke. The company's annual report needed to help doctors understand the cutting-edge technology, while communicating the financial picture to potential investors. Facts were presented in a graphic way to enhance readability.
KBDA

"**Design, initially, is knowing how to ask the right questions.**" —David Macaulay

This exhibit for Brigham Young University's athletic hall was designed to accommodate frequent updates and additions to exhibit materials. (See case study on page 216.)
Infinite Scale Design Group

"Information design is still to some degree the prisoner of an old either/or paradigm in which words and images exist in completely separate domains of use." —Robert E. Horn

Review Content While in Development. Once the client provides you with the content, review it carefully:

- Do you have all the pieces of the puzzle? Is the content complete and written in a thorough manner? If the original content is vague, it may be difficult or impossible to create clear information design around it.

- Is the messaging on target? Based on everything you've learned from prior conversations, research, and analysis, does the content feel authentic to the previously stated goals?

- Has the messaging been prioritized for the audience(s)? Here is where you can reference your personas, audience analysis, and research. Is the tone on target? Does the tone fit the client's brand?

- Is the content final and approved? If not, can word counts be provided? At this point, it's critical to have a sense of the depth and breadth of the content so that you can determine the best design approach and format. It's hard to know how to design a piece when you don't know if you're dealing with 500 or 5,000 words.

Conclusion: Master Content Wranglers Make Better Designers. Even though content wrangling may appear to be more work than you bargained for, in the end, several benefits emerge as a result of being involved in this part of the process. If you're naturally curious and drawn to information design, you probably already have an affinity for content. Whether you're a content junkie or an unsuspecting designer who's been thrown into an information design quagmire, staying on top of the content development process helps you:

- Eliminate surprises that can sneak up on you when you're already knee-deep into the project.

- Design effective solutions that are well organized and on target.

- Cement client relationships. Getting down and dirty with content development provides added value to your client, and pulls you up the design food chain so you're perceived as much more than a decorator.

- Stay engaged. One of the great things about being a designer is learning about different worlds and ideas. Being part of content development allows you to fully engage your intellect during the process.

Additional Firepower. Some designers can find themselves overwhelmed by the idea of being asked to help resolve content issues. If you and your team have writing communication skills and bandwidth, you may be able to offer this as a billable service to your clients. Alternatively, you can partner with skilled writers and copy editors who can become key allies in the process. Not every good copywriter is adept at thinking through the complex issues inherent in information design projects. If you do seek out partners, look for writers whose particular skill sets and experience match the project requirements.

Planning for the Long Run. In the past, many design artifacts had an expected shelf life of several years, but now changing business and information needs means a shorter shelf life for many projects, and the need for frequent updates. For ever-evolving projects, such as websites, newsletters, or public information graphics, how will future updates be accomplished?

It's important to ascertain any content updating issues early in the project so you can make informed decisions about file formats and other logistics. Here are some good questions to ask about content updating:

- Throughout the project, who will be responsible for managing this content, getting final approvals, organizing the drafts or revisions, and proofing?

- How often will the content need to be updated?

- What type of content will need to be updated? Just text or images also?

This website was built using a custom content management system allowing the client to continually update the site. (See case study on page 172.)
Hello Design

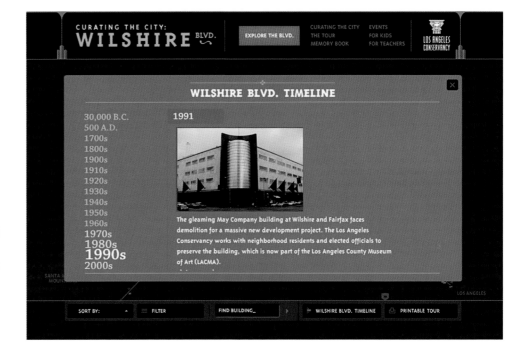

**MICA'S CURRICULUM OFFERS A
UNIQUE BALANCE OF**

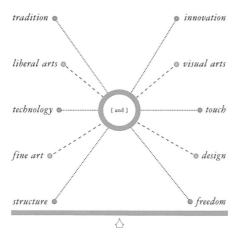

tradition

liberal arts

technology [and] *touch*

fine art *design*

structure *freedom*

innovation

visual arts

*Your learning at MICA will take place in the studio,
in conversations with accomplished faculty and your peers, and in a
range of real-world experiences.*

Your four years at MICA will provide a balance of structure and freedom, disciplined, rigorous study
and opportunities to take risks, explore your unique vision—laying a groundwork for a life of continual
exploration and achievement. At MICA, you'll gain the intellectual foundation, technical mastery, critical
insights, and creative vision that will give you an advantage in this fascinating, exciting world.

---

a solid foundation program
that prepares you for success
at MICA by offering both
the technical and conceptual
groundwork for your major

intellectual challenge through
the liberal arts core curriculum
and opportunities for deeper
study through liberal arts
majors and minors

a major in which you'll
develop technical expertise
and conceptual sophistication
in your discipline

career preparation—intern-
ships, alumni networking,
career-focused courses and
seminars—to help you build
a toolkit of professional skills
and real-world experience for
success after graduation

studio concentrations that
offer coherent programs of
study to complement your
major, expand your career
options

a senior thesis program in
which you'll make meaningful
connections between art-
making tand theory and focus
on producing a significant
body of work

structure

&

freedom

a curriculum that minimizes
barriers among disciplines and
encourages collaboration

flexibility to cross disciplines,
combine mediums, and
experiment in art-making

opportunities to experience
other cultures during a summer
or a semester of study abroad

a generous number of electives
in your major that let you take
advantage of the wide array of
courses offered by MICA's studio
and liberal arts departments

coursework that lets you explore
the connections between art and
music, science, critical writing,
literature, entertainment, and
community involvement

courses at Baltimore-area
universities like Johns Hopkins
that allow you to explore
additional academic interests—
from foreign languages and
anthropology to entrepreneur-
ship and environmental science

independent study options
and self-designed majors and
minors

**JAMILAH ABDUL-SABUR ▷ FRESHMAN
PHOTOGRAPHY MAJOR / VIDEO CONCENTRATION**

*Jamilah Abdul-Sabur
is a from Miami,
Florida. She attended
Dr. Michael M. Krop
Senior High. She is a
member of the Black
Student Union,
Channel Organics,
Ballet Club, RevCon,
and participates in
the Johns Hopkins
Breakdancing Club.
Her work was featured
in an exhibition at the
Maryland State
Senate Office Building
in Annapolis during
the Maryland
General Assembly's
2006 session, and she
was selected for the
two-week Off the
Wall Experimental
Lab residency at
Diaspora Vibe Gallery
in Miami for the
summer after her
freshman year, where
her solo exhibition
received a positive
review in the Miami
New Times.*

My foundation classes, especially Drawing with Bob Salazar and
Elements of Visual Thinking with Chris Whittey, helped me learn
where I wanted to go with my work. I realized that my tendency is to
work cinematically. Bob was very encouraging, and in his class, I developed my skills in video and visual production. I turned in a video for
my drawing final. That project helped me decide I want to pursue film
school after MICA. In Elements, I explored painting and sculpture for
the first time. Chris had very high expectations for us, and he pushed
us to explore, which led me to incorporate video and sculpture. Video
installation work is something that I plan to develop in the future.

*My work often has a political, environmental,
or social justice focus, picking up on the
activism that's always been important to me.*

In high school, I did 1,200 hours of community service with everything
from Aftershool Pre-Rest or to Greenpeace. At MICA, I organized
a monthly social justice film and discussion series in the Commons
Courthouse. With the breakdancing club, I interact with students from
Hopkins, the University of Baltimore, the University of Maryland, and
Morgan State University. Breakdancing has become an inspiration in my
life and artwork. I've also been to D.C., Virginia, Philadelphia, and New
York several times for art exhibitions, music shows, and break-dancing
competitions. I've been able to network and establish connections—not
just at MICA and in Baltimore, but throughout the East Coast.

Coming from Miami, I had to make a lot of adjustments, but I
love Baltimore, which is a progressive city, and I'm excited to be a part
of that. I've met a lot of artists in the arts and garden involved in the
break-dancing and music scenes. I saw Ravi Shankar (the "godfather
of world music") live at the Meterhoff Symphony Hall. Baltimore has
eclectic food. Charles Street, which is very close to campus, is one of
my favorite places—I got to try Afghani and Nepalese food for the first
time there.

- Can a non-designer make the updates easily, or will they require professional typesetting and design to ensure the integrity of the piece?

- Who will be responsible for gathering or creating material for content updates?

- Will the people updating the content have (or need) access to the software you are using to create the original files?

- Will multiple users be needed to update the design/information? Is there a workflow process in place to ensure the updates are made correctly and in a timely manner?

- What are the skill sets of the people updating the content? Will they need to be trained?

- How will the updated designs be produced? Will they need to be reprinted or published online? Will this require additional assistance from a printer or a technical development team?

People absorb information in various ways. For this art and design school catalog, content is displayed using multiple methods: illustrations, photographs, captions, diagrams, sidebars, as well as excellent use of pull quotes. The combination of information layout types makes for a very intriguing sense of pacing for the entire piece.
Rutka Weadock Design

Is It Bigger Than a Breadbox? "Form factor" is a term used in computing and engineering to describe size, format, shape, packaging, or housing of devices and mechanisms. We find ourselves appropriating the term to refer to design projects as well. There are plenty of considerations to take into account when deciding on the final "form factor" for an information design piece.

- The final form may not be what you first thought. For instance, you may have started out thinking of the project as a printed brochure, but discover your client's audiences will be more likely to access the information online.

- How will budget implications influence the format? Are there printing budgets, programming budgets, or content updating budgets to take into account? Are there mailing costs? For example, a square-format mailer will result in extra postage charges for the client— good to know.

- Are assumptions about the format hindering your ability to move in the right direction? Sometimes the client has a particular format in mind for a deliverable. It's also possible that a practical requirement has been assumed that later turns out to be inconsequential.

- The frequency with which the content needs to be updated should be a major consideration for the form factor.

"There is no such thing as objectivity. Even acts as simple and seemingly innocent as organizing data are subjective. Indeed, organizing data and the creating of information may have a profound impact on its meaning." —Nathan Shedroff

The Creative Brief

WHAT IS A CREATIVE BRIEF?

The creative brief is a short document (that's why they call it a brief) that typically runs anywhere from two to ten pages, depending on the scope of the project. This document outlines the pertinent information about the project so that the entire team has a clear sense of the project's background and goals.

WHY CREATE A CREATIVE BRIEF?

Creative briefs are nothing new to the world of communications and design. These documents have been around forever in the ad agency world. The same reason an ad agency would create a brief for an ad campaign applies to any design project: It's important to have a good plan. Information design projects, in particular, tend toward the kind of complexity that makes having a thoughtfully crafted creative brief especially helpful.

Too many projects proceed without the benefit of a clearly defined road map for the team. Without explicitly clear directions for how to move forward, information design project teams often find themselves either floundering or going full steam ahead

Good is a magazine that provides a platform for the ideas, people, and businesses that are driving change in the world. In a recurring section called "Transparency," *Good* features a self-described "graphical exploration of the data that surrounds us." Information graphics for each issue are created by different design firms, so Open, the firm responsible for the initial publication design, developed a creative brief to document and convey the most important aspects of the magazine's mission and personality.
Open

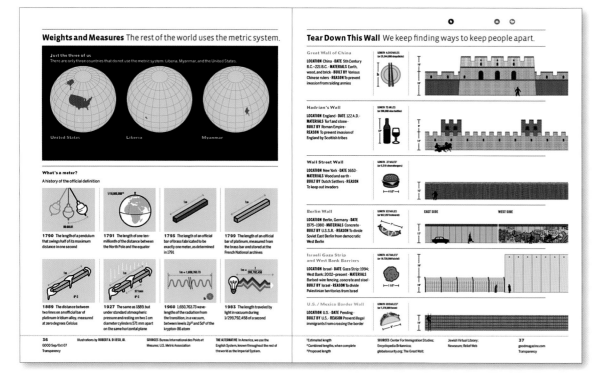

(possibly in the wrong direction) while the clock ticks and budgets drain away.

Let's say you've successfully set the stage for your project. You've spent time with the client and have a working understanding of their overall history and goals for their company and for the specific project at hand. Before you jump into the deep end and begin work on the project itself, it's time to document what you've learned so far.

CREATIVE BRIEF CONTENT: A SOURDOUGH STARTER KIT

There is apparently some debate in the design community (who knew?) over what makes for the perfect creative brief. There is debate over appropriate page count. Some people say, "It must be no longer than one page." There is debate over the brief's target audience. Some say, "The brief is the means by which you manage client expectations." Many others believe that the perfect creative brief speaks directly to the creative team and its process. Our thinking is that the perfect creative brief is tailored to the project and the team who needs to use it.

WHO NEEDS IT AND WHY?

Many times, the members of your design team haven't been in initial project meetings. They have no prior knowledge of the client or project. You could hold meetings, send emails, and verbally discuss what you know—all good. But what if you forget something or leave out critical bits of info?

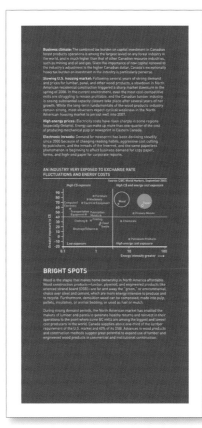

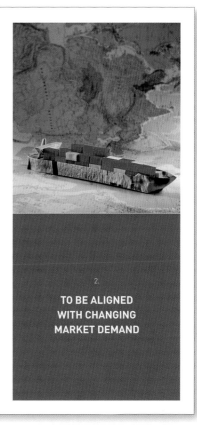

↑ Informed by clearly defined project goals, the annual review for Forest Products Association of Canada makes excellent use of subheads, diagrams, and interesting custom photos that illustrate key concepts.
McMillan

Because of the creative brief, Smart Design knew that one challenge in designing packaging is that retailers often take products out of the box for floor display. Smart Design created a sophisticated approach with a label affixed to the product itself, identifying the product and giving potential buyers an overview of product benefits. (See case study on page 128.)
Smart Design

The creative brief acts as a single point of communication to ensure that everyone is on the same page as the project moves forward. In addition, the brief can spark creative juices and get them flowing.

Design Team Reference. Projects start and stop due to unforeseeable events. Team members come and go. People are often working on several projects simultaneously. Even if you wanted to memorize all key project info, who has the time or mental bandwidth? A creative brief can be a repository for the critical, practical, and inspirational information you know you'll reference repeatedly. The brief is "the source" for project requirements and should be used as a benchmark to make sure the creative work is on target.

Client Approval and Feedback. The client should give attention and final approval to the creative brief before any work begins, to guarantee that the project is off to a good start.

The brief should echo the client's key points that you heard during conversations with them. In responding to the brief, the client can help you correct the course, vet your ideas and assertions, and help you home in on what's important to them.

In addition, the client can use the brief to get critical internal buy-in or feedback, and to gather input from people who, while not directly involved with the project, are nevertheless key players behind the scenes.

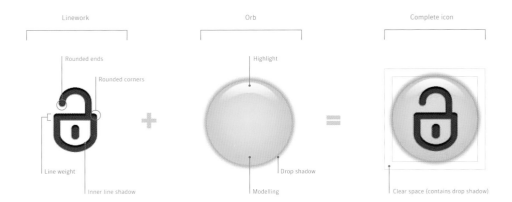

Linework — Rounded ends, Rounded corners, Line weight, Inner line shadow

Orb — Highlight, Drop shadow, Modelling

Complete icon — Clear space (contains drop shadow)

Comprehensive guidelines helped the in-house design team extend Symantec's new icon system.
MetaDesign

For Some Eyes Only. Some creative briefs are more detailed than others, depending on the complexity of the job, communication challenges, and the needs of the team. The document truly can be whatever you need it to be. For example, there may be times where you decide to create a "special edition" or version of the creative brief for your internal design team. There may be details that you don't want to highlight in the official brief that can really help your team understand the finer points of the project landscape. There may be client quirks, likes, dislikes, biases, past history, or even political agendas that would be useful to know as key design decisions are mapped out. An internal version of the creative brief can give your team the "inside scoop" about the client or project.

Bottom line: There's simply no right or wrong way to do it. What's important is that the creative brief captures the critical information so that the people who need it are "on the same page." Also critical: Get sign-off on the brief from your client to make sure your understanding of the project is accurate and complete.

Client Peace of Mind. Once approved, the brief can help put the client's mind at ease while the designers cloister themselves away and get down to the task of designing. As the creative process ensues over the course of several days or weeks, the client team knows there is a plan, has participated in the creation of that plan, and has a document that serves as a concrete reminder while they eagerly await the results of your genius.

TYPICAL CREATIVE BRIEF CONTENT

A typical creative brief breaks down information into four general categories: client information, project information, project goals and requirements, and project logistics.

Client Information. Include the client's full company name, number of years in business, noteworthy business accomplishments, whether a regional or national organization, and so on.

Client Sector. Give a bit of information about the client's business or industry. How competitive is their marketplace? Has their industry gone through particular changes lately?

Competitor Information. List your client's top three to five competitors and give a brief overview of each competitor's strengths and weaknesses in relation to your client.

Intended Audiences. Who are the main audiences for this client? Is there a particular subset for the information design project?

The Business Context for the Project. A thorough creative brief will take the following into account:

- Why this project at this time for this client?

- Is there any history of the project that would be helpful to know?

- Have similar projects been undertaken for this client? Were they successful or not? Why?

Project Information

Project Overview. Ideally, this is a one- or two-sentence overview of the project.

Key Information and Hierarchy. It also helps to address these issues when writing an effective creative brief:

- What key pieces of information need to be conveyed to the audience with this project? Ideally, you and your client will have thought this through. (See "Wrangling Audience and Content" on page 36.) You can use the creative brief to distill key points about the project information and hierarchies, giving the

team a quick-reference guide to the most important elements of the project, and enabling them to make well-informed decisions about how these elements relate to each other in the context of the design.

- What is the tone for the project? For instance, when designing a brochure and hiring chart for an entirely new system of job hierarchies, the tone might need to take into account employee anxiety and resistance to change. A public transit guide addressed to children might have an entirely different tone from one designed for adults.

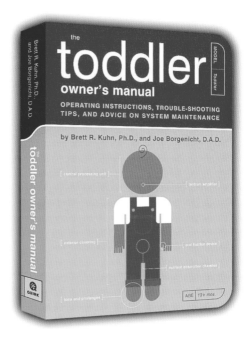

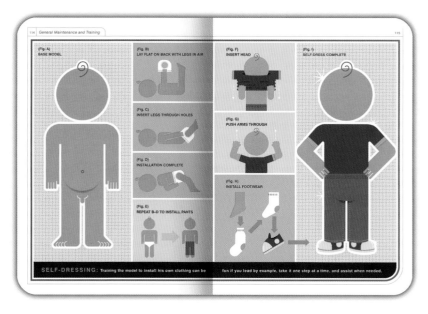

↑ This book's publisher was looking for an alternative to the cutesy baby book. The designers implemented an owner's manual aesthetic for the project. The book's atypical look and feel appeal to a male audience, a goal stated in the initial creative brief.
Headcase Design

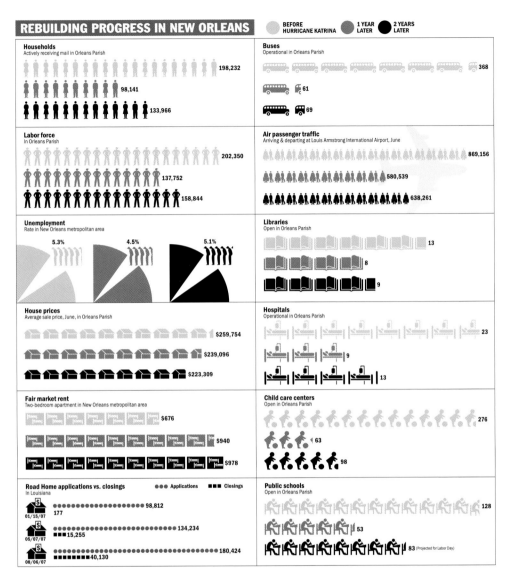

REBUILDING PROGRESS IN NEW ORLEANS

BEFORE HURRICANE KATRINA · 1 YEAR LATER · 2 YEARS LATER

Households
Actively receiving mail in Orleans Parish
198,232
98,141
133,966

Buses
Operational in Orleans Parish
368
61
69

Labor force
In Orleans Parish
202,350
137,752
158,844

Air passenger traffic
Arriving & departing at Louis Armstrong International Airport, June
869,156
580,539
638,261

Unemployment
Rate in New Orleans metropolitan area
5.3%
4.5%
5.1%

Libraries
Open in Orleans Parish
13
8
9

House prices
Average sale price, June, in Orleans Parish
$259,754
$239,096
$223,309

Hospitals
Operational in Orleans Parish
23
9
13

Fair market rent
Two-bedroom apartment in New Orleans metropolitan area
$676
$940
$978

Child care centers
Open in Orleans Parish
276
63
98

Road Home applications vs. closings
In Louisiana
● ● ● Applications   ■ ■ ■ Closings
01/15/07
98,812
177
05/07/07
134,234
15,255
08/06/07
180,424
40,130

Public schools
Open in Orleans Parish
128
53
83 (Projected for Labor Day)

↑ This *New York Times* infographic successfully simplifies an extremely complex story for the paper's target audience of busy readers. (Data provided by Amy Liu at the Brookings Institution.)
Nigel Holmes

SOMETIMES IT'S NOT EVEN CALLED A CREATIVE BRIEF

Funnel Incorporated takes a different approach to the creative brief. For one thing, they don't call it a creative brief at all. To them, it's a "shared understanding" document. Principal Lin Wilson explains:

"The title is very important because what we deliver is understanding—that's the common thread through all our work. Funnel has a tool that collects factual information and client goals. So the title is important, as is the series of questions. The most important are the first three.

"The first question is: What are the challenges to overcome?

"The second question is our point of difference from a typical design firm. We're asking what people are not understanding. The client is calling us for a reason and that might be because of confusion.

"The third question is about who the audience is: 'Is it your grandmother or is it a PhD?' These are super important to creating this kind of work."

When *TIME* magazine decided to reinvent itself, the design team drafted a creative brief with the following goal: Create a newsweekly that people would want to read. Bold photography and typography create a sense of gravitas and impact. (See case study on page 136.)
Pentagram Design

"There are an infinite number of journeys to take through the design of understanding."

—Richard Saul Wurman

Project Goals and Requirements

- What's the problem to solve?

- Where are the opportunities?

- How will success be measured?

- Are there any known issues or obstacles in the way of reaching project goals?

- What are the technical requirements? Is there existing technology that will need to be integrated?

- What are the creative requirements?

- Are there existing brand guidelines?

- Is there any other quirky information that can be helpful (colors the client hates, sacred cows, etc.)?

Project Logistics

Specific List of Deliverables. State the deliverables, as you understand them (including page counts, document sizes, file types, and so on).

Overview of the Project Team. Include key players on the client and design team sides. Clearly define roles and responsibilities. Determine who signs off on deliverables.

Key Dates. A detailed project schedule can be provided separately, but, by all means, list out the key dates you already know about.

Budget/Hours. Include an overview of hours allocated to the project, ideally by project phase.

WHO WRITES THE BRIEF?

Typically the person who's had the most contact with the client during the project start-up phase writes the brief. This could be the project manager, the account manager, or even the creative director or designer. Ideally, whoever writes the brief should be:

- Informed about the project details. This person should have first-hand experience with the client or at the very least have access to detailed meeting notes.

- A good writer. A creative brief needs to capture a lot of information in just a few pages. Writing style should be succinct but engaging enough keep the creative team from nodding off to sleep. The writing should wake up, fire up, and inspire the creatives.

THE CREATIVE BRIEF IN ACTION

It's worth the time you spend writing a creative brief. Done right, the approved document isn't just created for posterity. It can "ground" your design decisions at every step along the way. When you're ready to present to the client, reintroduce the brief to jog everyone's memories. Explain your design decisions as they map to key points in the brief. This way, when the clients are responding to the work and making design choices, they're doing so from a strategic point of view, as opposed to just a gut, or personal, response.

→ The Wonder of Reading, a non-profit organization, needed an effective fundraising brochure. The creative brief outlined the main goal for the piece: quickly convey the critical need to rebuild libraries in Los Angeles' public schools. By focusing on hard-hitting statistics and an evocative photo of a nearly empty library shelf, this spread conveyed more than paragraphs of text ever could.
KBDA

> California's children face a reading crisis.

> Literacy and education experts rank California last in the nation in the quality of its school libraries.

> California spends only three percent of what other states spend, on average, to support their school libraries.

> Our public elementary school libraries fail to meet our children's needs. Outdated design, limited opening hours, and paltry book collections severely hamper the ability of our children to acquire essential reading skills and to enjoy reading.

Personas and Scenarios

PERSONAS: IMAGINING USERS

> "You know you've been bitten by the information design bug when you begin to understand that the power of information design lies in the way it can be used to help people, to make their lives easier and better by providing serious, even life-saving communication."
>
> —Robert Swinehart

If successful information design requires a thorough understanding of and commitment to the audience, creating personas (sometimes also referred to as user profiles) is an easy and fun way to walk a mile in the shoes of your users.

During the initial research phase, you and your client identified target audiences. As you move into design development, well thought-out user profiles detail the relevant information about the personalities and expectations of representative members of your audience. User profiles provide a touchstone for the project team to make sure that design choices are aligned with user needs and expectations.

So while you may have identified your target audience as working mothers in their forties, having a persona for one particular working mother in her forties is infinitely more useful. Giving depth and details to the user's character helps you see the target audience member type as a full person with a wide range of needs and expectations. The idea is to be able to imagine fully how a particular user will interact with your design.

Cost-conscious, Yet Surprisingly Effective. How do you learn about a user or set of users and their needs and expectations? One can spend the time and budget seeking out and interviewing real people who fit a project's user demographic and then distill that information into real-world user profiles. However, the simplest, most cost-effective method of generating user profiles is to formulate them yourself based on research, common sense, and overall project know-how.

In the pragmatic world of information design, it may seem odd to be prompted to invent imaginary users the way you might have invented imaginary friends when you were five. Nevertheless, invented users can be a budget-conscious, time-sensitive, and extremely valuable device to help you and your team make decisions about the project at hand. Of course, you can't just haphazardly invent any old user. It's a good bet that Plimmy—the imaginary, orange, 7-foot (2.1 m) dragon who protected you from the mean kids on the kindergarten playground—will not assist you at all in your project efforts. This chapter outlines a general methodology to assist you in the process of creating personas that are relevant and useful to your project.

What Is a Persona and How Many Will You Need? A persona is a brief profile of a typical user that outlines specific personality attributes, desires, needs, habits, and capabilities. Often fictional, a persona can be a composite, or representative of a typical user (rather than an actual real-world user). If your audience encompasses

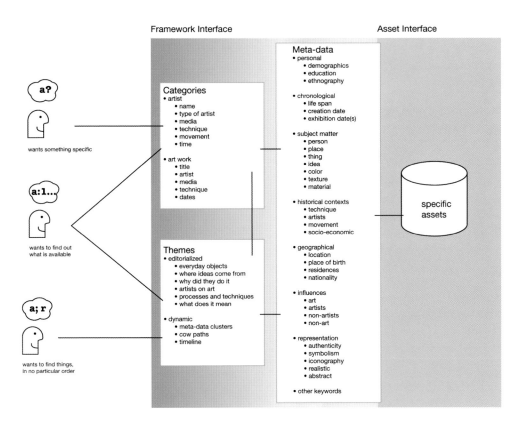

Framework Interface

Asset Interface

Categories
- artist
  - name
  - type of artist
  - media
  - technique
  - movement
  - time
- art work
  - title
  - artist
  - media
  - technique
  - dates

Themes
- editorialized
  - everyday objects
  - where ideas come from
  - why did they do it
  - artists on art
  - processes and techniques
  - what does it mean
- dynamic
  - meta-data clusters
  - cow paths
  - timeline

Meta-data
- personal
  - demographics
  - education
  - ethnography
- chronological
  - life span
  - creation date
  - exhibition date(s)
- subject matter
  - person
  - place
  - thing
  - idea
  - color
  - texture
  - material
- historical contexts
  - technique
  - artists
  - movement
  - socio-economic
- geographical
  - location
  - place of birth
  - residences
  - nationality
- influences
  - art
  - artists
  - non-artists
  - non-art
- representation
  - authenticity
  - symbolism
  - iconography
  - realistic
  - abstract
- other keywords

specific assets

a?

wants something specific

a:1...

wants to find out
what is available

a; r

wants to find things,
in no particular order

This process document for the Making Sense of Modern Art (MSOMA) kiosk at San Francisco Museum of Modern Art describes a framework that establishes relationships between content and users.
Method

The MSOMA kiosk's final user interface design incorporates user wants and needs that were identified during the project's planning stages. The modular interface highlights individual artists, as well as content types such as guided tours, videos, and timelines. Information is organized so that users with varied goals can explore the content in the way that best suits their browsing habits.
Method

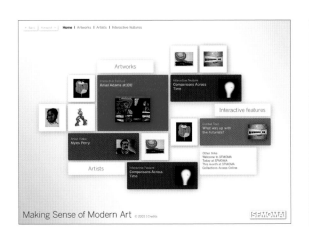

⬆ This persona includes a photo of the user, which lends a sense of reality to the entire piece. Particular user goals for this character are highlighted with a quote, which effectively gives the user a voice to communicate what the user type really wants.
Matter

many kinds of users, you'll probably need to create a series of personas that reflect the range in audience types. Most projects require about three to five personas.

How Do You Create Personas? First, you need to identify your main audience types. Ask your client for specific details. Talking with the client about their users can both clarify the audience list and raise new questions about the types of users the client wants to target. Research the client's business landscape for further ideas and information about the user base.

Next, create a short list of specific attributes for your most common audience types. Again, work with the client to hone the list of attributes. Some of these attributes will be more general, such as age, gender, profession, geography, and education. Some of the attributes will be more specific to the project, like how often the person might use the "product," whether the person is comfortable with new technology, or whether the person likes to read.

Sometimes the demographics (age, gender, and socioeconomic status) are less important than the psychographics (personality, values, attitudes, interests, or lifestyles).

Who Creates the Personas? A single person on the team, such as the designer, the information architect, or the project manager, can create the personas. However, a group work session with the design team and the client team is one of the best ways to generate a set of personas. Not only do you gather more creative input during a collaborative process, but the act of creating personas is a great team-building exercise at the start of a project.

The client team, especially at project inception, will generally know more about their users than you will. On the other hand, you, as the designer, will often ask valuable questions, and even question certain client assumptions. For example, when discussing a Web project, the design team might inquire about the user's computer equipment and home environment, and how that might impact browsing habits and time spent online.

So go ahead and gather the team in a room with a whiteboard, coffee, and a few snacks, and have a group work session to come up with each of the personas based on the predetermined set of user attributes and criteria.

Document Your Efforts. Once you've gathered all the data for your personas, create a document featuring the fruits of your labor. Each persona should include all the pertinent criteria and attributes. It also helps to have a picture of each character. Give each persona a name, too. Giving each persona a name brings the user to life, encourages empathy, and makes the discussion infinitely more personal.

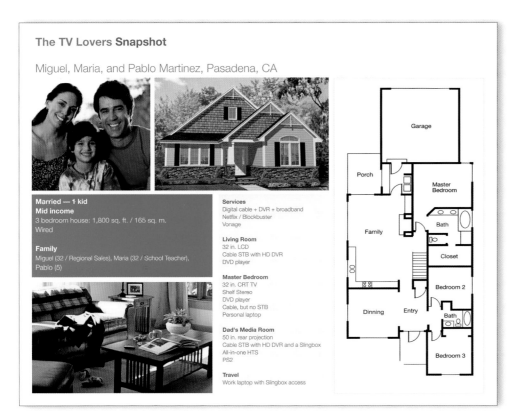

The TV Lovers Snapshot

Miguel, Maria, and Pablo Martinez, Pasadena, CA

Married — 1 kid
Mid income
3 bedroom house: 1,800 sq. ft. / 165 sq. m.
Wired

Family
Miguel (32 / Regional Sales), Maria (32 / School Teacher),
Pablo (5)

Services
Digital cable + DVR + broadband
Netflix / Blockbuster
Vonage

Living Room
32 in. LCD
Cable STB with HD DVR
DVD player

Master Bedroom
32 in. CRT TV
Shelf Stereo
DVD player
Cable, but no STB
Personal laptop

Dad's Media Room
50 in. rear projection
Cable STB with HD DVR and a Slingbox
All-in-one HTS
PS2

Travel
Work laptop with Slingbox access

Garage

Porch

Master Bedroom

Bath

Family

Living Room

Closet

Bedroom 2

Dinning

Entry

Bath

Bedroom 3

This persona by Method gives details about potential users.
Method

Even if the project isn't Web-based or technology-related, it might be interesting to know how your persona interacts with such devices. For a cookbook design, you may want to know which cooking websites, magazines, and cookbooks the user likes.

Details give your persona dimension and character. It's often helpful to include information that shows how the user relates to your project or client goals. Personas can be as specific as you need them to be. If it helps to know exactly what Joe thinks about your product, service, or information design issue, by all means, give the guy an opinion about it.

Information about personality can also help you make decisions about your information design. For example, if your key users are impatient by nature and, thus, only want the broad strokes and "big picture" information, then your information design choices will differ significantly than if your users are very patient, literate, and detail-oriented in approach.

When the personas are fully cataloged, distribute the document to the team.

How Do You Use Personas? Once you have the personas in hand, it's easier to understand the audiences and prioritize them. It helps to rank the importance of each persona in terms of project needs and goals. Not only do you have a set of representative users in hand, but you now know which users and their needs are the most critical.

Having personas as a reference while you work on the project helps to create empathy and a deeper understanding for user needs and how the particular audience types might respond to your design. Personas can be quite useful in making distinctions and choosing between design options. For

→ This early process document by Method shows the details and functionality scenario for the software and hardware for a phone system, including a visual representation of the concept.
Method

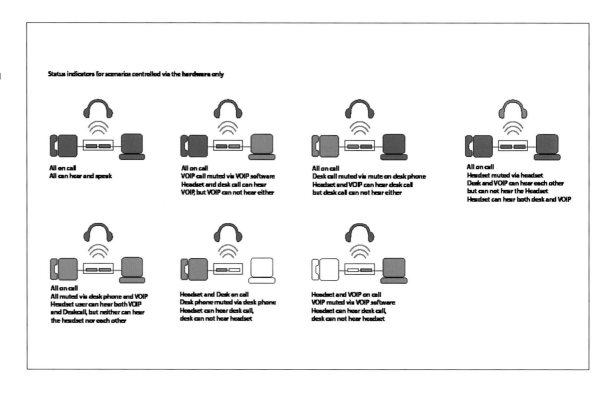

Status indicators for scenarios controlled via the hardware only

All on call
All can hear and speak

All on call
VOIP call muted via VOIP software
Headset and desk call can hear
VOIP, but VOIP can not hear either

All on call
Desk call muted via mute on desk phone
Headset and VOIP can hear desk call
but desk call can not hear either

All on call
Headset muted via headset
Desk and VOIP can hear each other
but can not hear the Headset
Headset can hear both desk and VOIP

All on call
All muted via desk phone and VOIP
Headset user can hear both VOIP
and Deskcall, but neither can hear
the headset nor each other

Headset and Desk on call
Desk phone muted via desk phone
Headset can hear desk call,
desk can not hear headset

Headset and VOIP on call
VOIP muted via VOIP software
Headset can hear desk call,
desk can not hear headset

instance, if you know your most important demographic is a hip, urban, artsy audience of 25- to 35-year-old females, you may choose a different design than if your audience is a hip, urban, artsy audience of 25- to 35-year-old females who have children. The overall demographics and personality attributes may be very similar. However, the specifics of the personas shed light on key differences that can influence user behavior in a pronounced way.

You'll be surprised at how often clients and design team members will refer back to the personas when making decisions throughout the length of the project.

SCENARIOS SHOW PERSONAS AT WORK

Personas are like actors. Now that you've got your cast in place, it's a good idea to have your imaginary users act out the process of interacting with the information design in question.

Scenarios help you identify specific patterns in how users interact with information design. Like the personas themselves, scenarios help you confirm that your design satisfies the needs of the target audience.

A scenario can be a story written in narrative form or another form such as a flowchart or diagram. Scenarios can be very specifically related to one task flow such as how a user completes a specific transaction with an online system to purchase a building permit. Or scenarios can be more general in telling the story of how a particular user interacts with the system over time and through a variety of touch points. You can decide how general or how specific your scenario needs to be depending on the complexity of your project and your need for user information about the project.

A thoughtful and considered approach to information design can make all the difference in the success of a project. The following sections explore best practices in the field today and give practical tips and advice on creating planning documents and testing your design.

PROCESS: PROTOTYPES AND TESTING

3

Structural Overviews

GUIDES TO UNDERSTANDING
THE BIG PICTURE

Because information design projects often have a deeper level of complexity and volume of information than other design projects, you will probably need to create one or more supporting documents to aid you in the process before you begin visual design.

Supporting structural-overview documents such as sitemaps and page maps (both of which are, in essence, flowcharts) can help you gather and organize information elements and help you figure out information flow. It's true that flowcharts and other overview charts can seem dry, boring, or even confusing to the untrained eye. However, in cases where an information design project contains many parts or levels of information, a flowchart or other diagram that visually outlines the structure of the project can often be a huge help in creating order out of apparent chaos.

WHAT IS A SITEMAP?

With projects that include very deep layers of information (such as websites, exhibitions, complex publications, or other information-dense projects), you'll be doing your visual design team a huge disservice if there is no overall map of the project from a structural point of view. Working on a complex project without a big-picture overview is enough to make even the most patient designers run screaming.

A sitemap or similar flowchart outlining all project components is one of the first documents you may need, and it should be created long before visual design begins.

Basically, the sitemap (or a similar overview map if you're working on something other than a website) should give a visual outline of all the components and informational elements of the project. It's a high-level, organized laundry list of everything that

> "Design, after all, has the unique capacity to shape information by emphasizing or understating, comparing or ordering, grouping or sorting, selecting or omitting, opting for immediate or delayed recognition, and presenting it in an entertaining fashion."
>
> —Paul Mijksenaar

➜ The use of a main navigation bar in the Nike investor relations microsite was determined by the overall sitemap, but this did not preclude designers from experimenting with several different designs for the home page.
KBDA

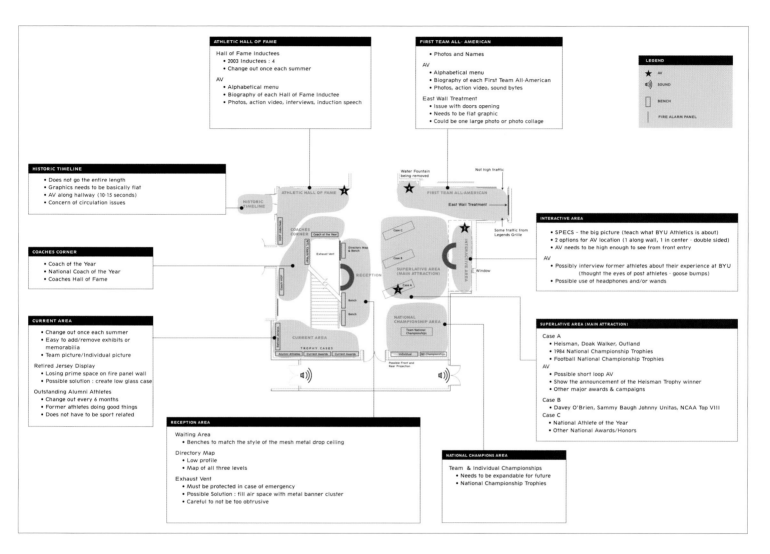

ATHLETIC HALL OF FAME

Hall of Fame Inductees
- 2003 Inductees : 4
- Change out once each summer

AV
- Alphabetical menu
- Biography of each Hall of Fame Inductee
- Photos, action video, interviews, induction speech

FIRST TEAM ALL- AMERICAN
- Photos and Names

AV
- Alphabetical menu
- Biography of each First Team All-American
- Photos, action video, sound bytes

East Wall Treatment
- Issue with doors opening
- Needs to be flat graphic
- Could be one large photo or photo collage

LEGEND

★ AV

◄)) SOUND

▢ BENCH

▢ FIRE ALARM PANEL

HISTORIC TIMELINE
- Does not go the entire length
- Graphics needs to be basically flat
- AV along hallway (10-15 seconds)
- Concern of circulation issues

COACHES CORNER
- Coach of the Year
- National Coach of the Year
- Coaches Hall of Fame

INTERACTIVE AREA
- SPECS – the big picture (teach what BYU Athletics is about)
- 2 options for AV location (1 along wall, 1 in center - double sided)
- AV needs to be high enough to see from front entry

AV
- Possibly interview former athletes about their experience at BYU (thought the eyes of post athletes - goose bumps)
- Possible use of headphones and/or wands

CURRENT AREA
- Change out once each summer
- Easy to add/remove exhibits or memorabilia
- Team picture/Individual picture

Retired Jersey Display
- Losing prime space on fire panel wall
- Possible solution : create low glass case

Outstanding Alumni Athletes
- Change out every 6 months
- Former athletes doing good things
- Does not have to be sport related

SUPERLATIVE AREA (MAIN ATTRACTION)

Case A
- Heisman, Doak Walker, Outland
- 1984 National Championship Trophies
- Football National Championship Trophies
AV
- Possible short loop AV
- Show the announcement of the Heisman Trophy winner
- Other major awards & campaigns
Case B
- Davey O'Brien, Sammy Baugh Johnny Unitas, NCAA Top VIII
Case C
- National Athlete of the Year
- Other National Awards/Honors

RECEPTION AREA

Waiting Area
- Benches to match the style of the mesh metal drop ceiling

Directory Map
- Low profile
- Map of all three levels

Exhaust Vent
- Must be protected in case of emergency
- Possible Solution : fill air space with metal banner cluster
- Careful to not be too obtrusive

NATIONAL CHAMPIONS AREA

Team & Individual Championships
- Needs to be expandable for future
- National Championship Trophies

This sitemap documents the content and site requirements for the first level of Brigham Young University's Student Athlete Center. The 10,000-square-foot (929 sq. m), three-level athletic hall of fame encapsulates 100 years of BYU sports. The plan helped the design team determine the best allocation of space for the exhibits. **Infinite Scale Design Group**

A streetscape enhancement project for the City of South Pasadena was designed to reinforce a sense of place and encourage pedestrian traffic. This map helped the community evaluate the proposed placement of sign types—destination wayfinding, historic documentation, and storytelling. (See page 73 for wireframe diagrams that show signage details.)
KBDA

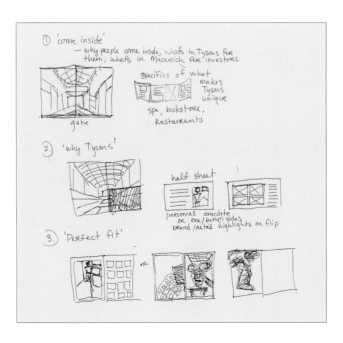

Similar to sitemaps, page maps are usually generated for complex print projects such as books and magazines. Page maps help the design and client teams understand the flow of a multipage piece and help the team come to an agreement about the ordering and hierarchy of information and the allocation of space for the entire piece at a macro level. This working page map captured, at a high level, the storytelling arc of the piece.
KBDA

should be included in the project. Sitemaps are foundational tools of information architecture, related to the master planning documents that architects have traditionally used when designing extremely complex building projects such as hospitals or university campuses.

HOW IS A SITEMAP USED?

Coherent Diagrams: Elegant Solutions. Sitemaps are most commonly found in the world of Web and interactive design. In this context, a sitemap is an invaluable tool in helping the project team figure out the overall site structure, navigation flow, and navigation nomenclature. A well-organized sitemap gives you an at-a-glance view of the entire site, with all its main sections, pages, and sublevel pages.

Organizing the data is the first step. Once the initial diagram is in place, components can be shuffled and reordered, and categories changed, all with the goal of meeting overall project objectives.

Sitemap-style documents aren't only useful for websites, although in terms of information design projects, they're most often used for deliverables that have an interactive, screen-based component. However, there are many other types of projects that might make use of a sitemap or similar flowchart. Interactive games, DVD menu sequences, museum exhibits, and even banking kiosk projects might be served by having a sitemap.

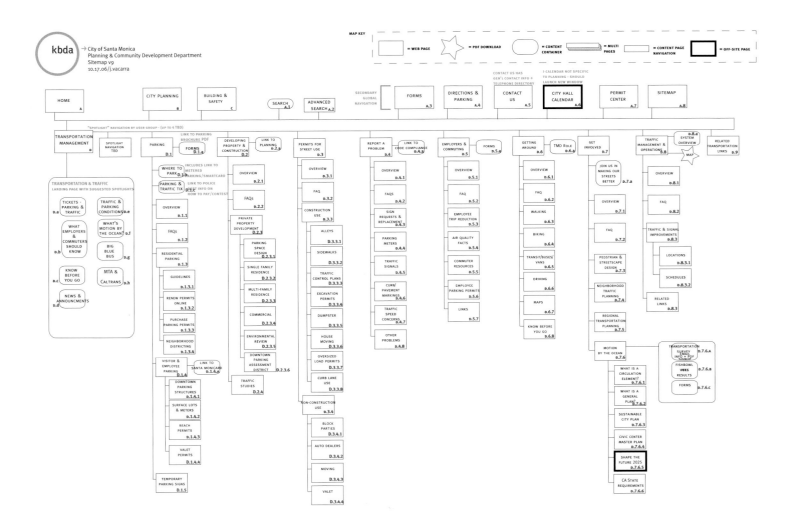

This is a standard sitemap for a Web project. Note how the map includes a key explaining the different diagrammatic elements on the map, such as which shape constitutes a Web page, which pages are actually PDF downloads, and which links lead someplace off the main site.

KBDA

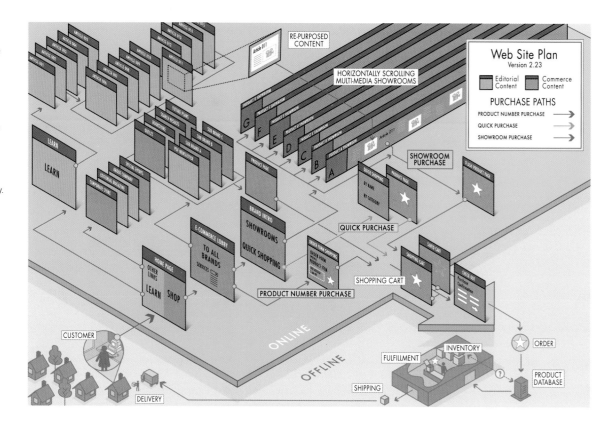

This sitemap created by Funnel Incorporated started out as a typical black-and-white flowchart with boxes and lines. To better communicate with the client's internal nontechnical audience, Funnel designed a 3-D diagram of the site from both the functional perspective and the perspective of three main customer profiles. This alternative sitemap is designed to be very user-friendly, with color coding and dimensionality. This more accessible and richly detailed approach enabled the client's internal team to understand, approve, and fund the solution for their site.
Funnel Incorporated

If you have a project with several layers of information, you could probably use a sitemap-style framework, especially if the project has multiple information flows or sequences that need to be mapped out. An innovative and thoughtful approach to an information design project in big-box retail, for example, could illuminate new approaches to customers' experiences of the aisles, shopping categories, and wayfinding in a store.

Sitemaps and Team Consensus. A sitemap helps ensure that a sound plan is approved and in place before the team proceeds to subsequent project phases of design,

programming, content development, and build-out. With design projects that include many layers of information, you definitely don't want to jump into the design phase without a solid framework. Designing a complex, information-intensive project without a plan tends to lead to haphazard solutions.

It's often said that the only constant is change, and this is especially true of information design projects. Having an organized map of the project allows you and the client to capture details about the project's evolution so you can plan for revisions and future versions of the design.

Discussion and Signoff. The sitemap, or another similar map/planning document, is often the first document the client will see after the creative brief. Clients may not understand the sitemap immediately and will probably need some handholding from you. That's okay. The point here is to catalog everything at a high level for the purpose of discussion with the client and team. At this point in the project, a lot could change in terms of the informational structure and content. Trust us, it's much better to change an elemental flowchart document than page after page of actual screen design.

"Designers can learn from library science. In trying to deliver information, what are the cognitive frameworks or resistances to absorbing information? We're always trying to make information delivery as painless and seamless as possible. Even to the point that the person has no conscious perception of how the information is being delivered." —Micki Breitenstein

Don't be surprised, however, if your sitemap goes through several iterations. Once the client and design team have a plan in front of them, they will have new ideas, discover opportunities, and debate options. The sitemap allows this discussion to take place in an organized fashion. Sitemaps can be revised and revised again. Several versions are often necessary and healthy for the project. Try not to start the next phase of the project before the sitemap is approved, though, or you could find yourself wasting precious hours revising more time-intensive design documents.

WHAT SHOULD A SITEMAP LOOK LIKE?

Sitemaps and similar flowchart overview documents can come in all shapes and sizes. There are probably infinite ways to create a sitemap or other map-type diagram. You can draw it using an illustration program or a flowchart program. You can create a simple index/listing in a word processing program. You can create a sitemap out of index cards displayed on a board. You can sketch one on a napkin. Sitemaps can be simple black-and-white diagrams. They can be animated or interactive if necessary. They can be 3-D models if you think that's useful. Hey, you can even make a sitemap out of modeling clay if that works for your project. Your project content and goals should guide you.

Whatever you need to communicate about the informational components of your project can be reflected in the sitemap. Like many maps and diagrams, a good sitemap might have a key to explain the meaning of certain map elements. Are there pieces of information that are different from the others? Let the sitemap show that. This chapter provides samples of some typical and not-so-typical sitemaps to give you an idea of how you might apply this type of document to your project.

Creating the Blueprints

> **"Psychologists and experts in the field of human perception tell us that human beings take in data through the senses and turn it into something that is memorable and has meaning. This can then become permanent knowledge. Designers have to find ways to make the information meaningful."**
>
> —Krzysztof Lenk

WIREFRAMES FLESH OUT A PROJECT

Big-picture overviews are extremely helpful and often necessary, but they may not allow for the level of detail that your team will need to determine the right approach for the visual design of the project. If the sitemap or structural overview is a kind of skeleton, wireframes add a bit more flesh and muscle. Like sitemaps, wireframes (sometimes also referred to as schematics) are often found in the worlds of environmental and interactive design, and are also used for complex print projects. Like sitemaps, wireframes are planning documents and, thus, are not concerned with

design details such as typography, shape, and color. At this point, you're still in the planning stages and using broad strokes.

Like a blueprint for a house, the wireframe acts as a detailed guideline for layout and functionality within the information design piece. With the sitemap, you generally figure out the hierarchy of information and determine the master plan for the piece. In essence, you decide which rooms will be included in the house, and the flow of traffic between them.

The wireframes begin to give shape to the structure and provide detail for all the rooms and features within the structure.

Funnel Incorporated's process includes preliminary whiteboard sketches done in work sessions with their clients to get a sense of the information flow and layout of a project. The sketching process happens before visual design begins and helps everyone "get the story right" in advance.
Funnel Incorporated

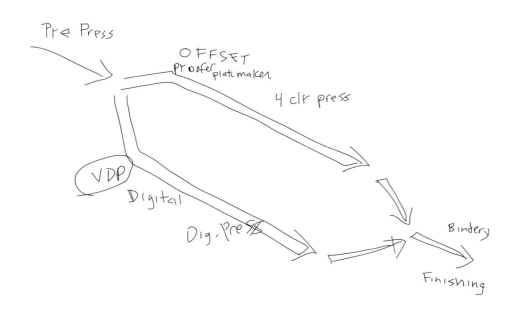

You begin by asking questions: Are all the rooms the same size or different? Does each room have the same function? How much wall space will there be? How much furniture do we need to accommodate in each room? How many doors and windows are there, and how do those doors and windows function? Are they standard doors, sliding doors, or French windows?

Wireframes map out which elements in the design are most and least important to determine the focal points for the design of the house. Which rooms are the central showcase areas for the house? Which part of a room is its focal point (fireplace, sofa, great work of art)? (Since this is a precursor to visual design, you won't have chosen the fireplace style, the sofa, or the art; you're just making the space for it. Wireframes allow you to plan without making specific choices about shape, color, or other visual components.)

DON'T BUILD WITHOUT A BLUEPRINT

While the sitemap or structural overview provides a bird's-eye view, wireframes flesh out the finer details of a complex information design project. They help answer questions: How much content will we need to consider as we create the design? What kinds of specific information do we need to design around? Do we need headers and subheaders for the content? How much main text is there? Are there pieces of related content that live alongside the main content but in a separate area of the layout? What other types of information does the design need to accommodate and how should we display that information? Will we need lists? Diagrams? Charts? Illustrations? Few, if any, of these issues can be planned

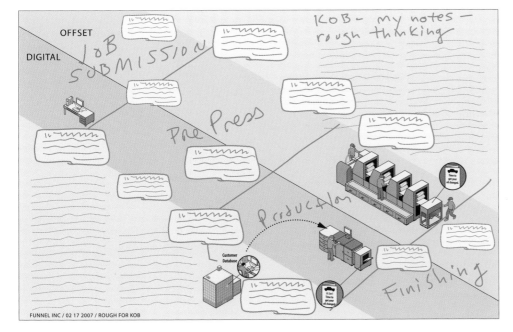

From the whiteboard sketch, designers then execute a rough sketch that introduces layout and look and feel without dealing specifically with all of the content that will be used in the final piece.
Funnel Incorporated

FUNNEL INC / 02 17 2007 / ROUGH FOR KOB

This final version of the Funnel design shows how preliminary elements of the sketch evolved into the end deliverable. Planning in advance helped to organize the complex information in terms of flow, hierarchy, layout, and storytelling.
Funnel Incorporated

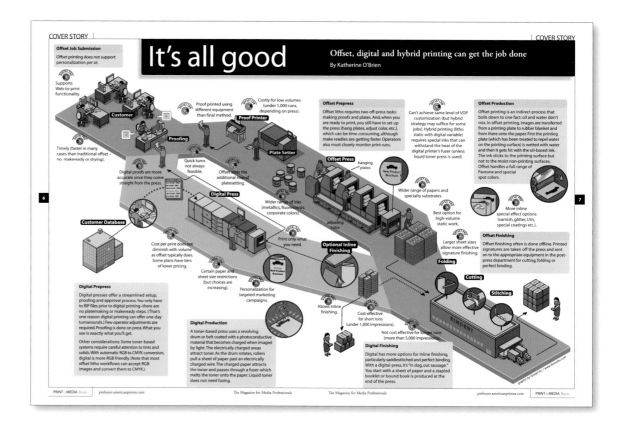

> **"Information is the beginning of meaning. Information is data put into context, with thought given to its organization and presentation."** —Nathan Shedroff

properly on a structural overview diagram like a sitemap. There's simply not enough detail in that kind of overview document. Wireframe sketches allow you to carefully envision all of these details.

A wireframe is, in a sense, a sketch that allows the design team and client to see a detailed view of how the content will be organized on just a few given pages or sections of your project. For websites, you might choose a series of representative site pages (often called page types) for your set of wireframe sketches. For instance, for a website, you might start with the home page and a few drill-down

pages. Book or magazine content sketches might show rough templates for how the typical feature or department content will be organized into headers, introduction text, body text, and sidebars.

Without wireframes, you can spend a lot of time and budget creating highly detailed design deliverables only to find that not all of the project parameters have been thought through. If you're designing a website home page based on three spotlight areas for content and suddenly the client wants five spotlights, it's much easier to revise and update a simple wireframe sketch than to rework a fully realized layout.

Wireframes help ensure your design planning is thorough and deliberate. By the time your team is ready to begin visual design, you'll have thought of most, if not all, of the issues related to the organization and display of the information you need to include in your project.

WHAT SHOULD A WIREFRAME LOOK LIKE?

Wireframe documents tend to look like their moniker: plain, wirelike drawings with basic text labels. Nothing too fancy. Nevertheless, there are no hard-and-fast rules for creating wireframes. You can draw them using a variety of tools and methods, depending on project content and goals. The main

goal is to catalog all the information in layout form but without spending time and thought applying any specific visual design elements.

Wireframes don't have to be ugly (Why should anything you create be ugly?), but it doesn't make sense to spend an inordinate amount of time making them beautiful. For one thing, people might wrongly assume your gorgeously nuanced wireframes are reflective of the final look and feel for the piece. Wireframes should be sketches that are clear, thorough, and free from extraneous graphic elements and details.

Some information designers use color in their wireframes sketches. If you use color, limit your palette to one or two colors that you use to emphasize certain information.

By primarily sticking to black and white or grayscale, you won't run the risk of confusing your clients into thinking they're looking at visual design deliverables. And you won't be inadvertently starting or pre-empting the visual design process before that phase has begun.

THE BEAUTY OF INTERPRETATION

Most of the time, wireframes will look absolutely nothing like the final design. And, ideally, during the next phase of the project when you present the visual design options, you will have diverse visual solutions that look radically different from each other, all based on the same set of wireframes.

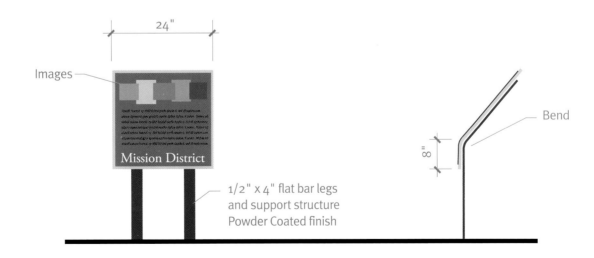

→ These content sketches were created in generic sign templates as part of the planning phase of the City of South Pasadena's streetscape enhancement project. The goal was to get the community to approve the content requirements for two proposed sign types before actual design commenced. (See the sitemap on page 66 for the structural overview of the Pasadena signage project.)
KBDA

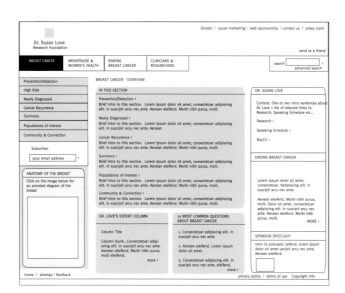

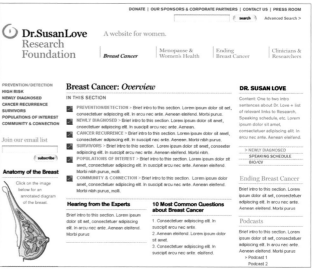

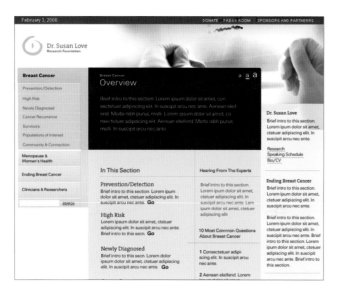

A wireframe (top left) was given to three different designers for the Dr. Susan Love Research Foundation website redesign project. The designers (David Handschuh, Keith Knueven, and Liz Burrill) each interpreted the wireframe quite differently, giving the client several options to choose from.
Jill Vacarra Design

Make It Just Real Enough. Wireframes should look enough like the final piece so a layperson can understand, with a little explanation, what they're looking at. As we've discussed, you don't have to come close to a final design at this stage. But, for example, if you're creating a website wireframe, you'll want to make the document look enough like a website so that the person gets the gist. You probably want to use the same dimensions as a typical Web screen and use some detailing to clarify navigational elements. If you're creating wireframes for signage, it helps to give the diagram a few recognizable visual cues, like a signpost or sign frame, to help viewers instantly understand that the sketch represents a sign.

ACHIEVING CLIENT CONSENSUS

Wireframes give you a way to map out the piece in advance and to reach team consensus regarding the form and content of your final design. The wireframe stage of a complex information design project can go through many, many iterations. Once you have team and client approval, the design team will then use the wireframe sketches as a detailed reference guide as they begin to address the visual design.

Continued Research with Wireframes. It's a really good idea to test key elements of your information design at the wireframe sketch stage with target audience members. Even before you've spent time and effort on the detailed visual aspects of the design, you can test your thinking.

The client and design team may be making assumptions that you can avoid if you ask end users for their feedback at this stage in the process.

By showing the wireframe sketches, you can ask users if they understand how the information in your project is categorized, organized, and named. You can find out if you've inadvertently made choices that cause confusion for users. Wireframes can allow you to find out quite a bit about how audiences will react to the information design piece even before you and your team have spent the time and budget on look and feel.

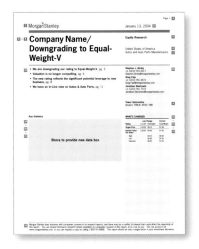
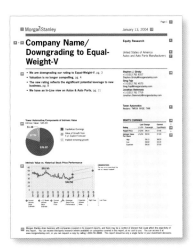
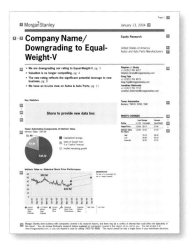

Carbone Smolan Agency worked to develop a comprehensive way for Morgan Stanley to publish their global equity research reports. After thorough research, CSA created wireframes to illustrate possible options for organizing the content. (See case study on page 124.)
Carbone Smolan Agency

Research and Testing

You've done your audience research. You know your users and have a good overall sense of what they will need when interacting with your design. You know your client's mission and goals for the project. Based on all of this initial research, you have chosen a direction for the project and have started the design process and made some headway. You may even have some innovative design solutions on the table. But how can you be sure that you're not designing just for yourself or in a vacuum? How can you confirm that important information is being effectively communicated?

DON'T GUESS, TEST!

Also referred to as usability testing, user testing is a bit of a misnomer because it implies that your users are being tested themselves when really it's the design that's being tested. Testing is really just another form of research. With the initial research, you set the direction, gather requirements, and lay the foundation for the project. Testing throughout the design development cycle ensures that the design becomes more and more focused toward getting it right. Testing is like having guardrails along the interstate. The guardrails aren't the actual road, but they make sure you don't drive off the cliff.

But testing shouldn't be a separate, isolated, and annoying step, an afterthought that no one wants to do or pay for. With user-centered design, you build the user feedback loop into your design process, right from the start.

"If you're going to inflict something, it's polite to see if it's useful. It's an act of a civil society to involve people to ensure that the outcome is useful." —David Sless

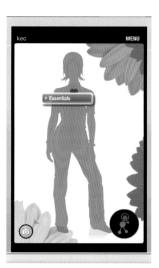

mEgo is a profiling tool for representing users across multiple social networks. Testers felt the first avatar graphic approach was too "young and cartoon-like." Testing also revealed that users did not understand that mEgo was interactive and that further content was available on rollover. mEgo created an alternate "silhouette avatar" that appealed to a wider range of ages. Tool tips were animated over the image to invite user interaction with the profile's content areas.
What's Next Interactive Inc.

RESIST THE URGE NOT TO TEST

Isn't testing expensive and time-consuming? These are two assumptions clients—and designers themselves—often make when deciding not to test. Sometimes a design team falls into the trap of thinking they'll convince the client to test after the project is well underway (or at the very end of the project, when many design decisions have already been made). At that point, however, introducing a testing phase will probably be seen as an unnecessary expense. The client has invested a lot of time and money in you

as a design expert. So why not just rely on your expertise? Everyone on the team has invested a great deal of time and energy in the current design solution. Testing for the very first time so late in the game seems like a chore. Worse yet, what if all that creativity and energy have been focused in the wrong direction? If there are problems, sometimes we just don't want to know.

Testing—especially informal testing—needn't have a huge impact on your overall timeframe for the project, if you build iterative testing into your process.

You can (and should) also conduct more formal user testing at the end of the project, but by that time you'll be testing a design that has already been through a process of refinement based on real user feedback.

Testing Saves Money. The value proposition of testing is that if you do it from the beginning, the project may cost a bit more, but it will end up saving money in the long run. The likelihood of "getting it right" in version 1.0 of your project will go up exponentially the more research testing you do.

← With environmental projects, it's imperative to test design decisions in context before final fabrication begins. In a signage project for the Salt Lake City Winter Olympic Games, for example, the design firm consistently reviewed full-scale mockups and materials on-site to make sure the scale and contrast levels of the graphic elements were effective.
Infinite Scale Design Group

Best Practices, Radical Simplification, and User-centered Design

Kathryn Campbell, principal of What's Next Interactive, provides strategic consulting, testing services, and user-centered design training. Campbell and her team use proven methodologies grounded in user research and business analytics while encouraging experimentation, creativity, and user-centric design for interactive projects.

How does radical simplification apply to the user-centric design process?

KC: We need to recognize the built-in tendency during concept development toward excessive sophistication. There is the inclination to look at what everyone else has done and say, "We want to include all that, plus everything we've ever tried, plus more."

Complexity often creates cognitive noise, preventing the user from focusing on the essential information you want to communicate. What are the must-have features? What can be cut? Create more division between the must-haves and the nice-to-haves.

What do you think of the notion of best practices in terms of usability?

KC: I have a lot of respect for Jakob Nielsen and other usability traditionalists. I respect that they base their thinking on research rather than so-called best practices in the marketplace. Often people define best practices as "other people do it." That's bull#@*! Show me the best practices that led to iPod!

How can we push the design envelope in the face of so-called best practices?

KC: One of the biggest disservices that usability traditionalists have done is they've bludgeoned people into thinking that if they design something different, it will be unusable. If you're recommending something significantly different than a typical approach, test it to see if it works. I've tested some incredibly nonstandard, progressive information design, but at the end of the interviews, users thought it was better and easier! If you're smart, you can make designs innovative and useful.

Are there any tried-and-true best practices?

KC: Some conventions hold true. The eye-tracking data that says the upper right is a bad place to put something important is absolutely true. People have become trained to search for left navigation on websites. If you put something in the upper right of a Web screen, you better be sure you use a technique, a color, something to call attention. We have many tools: visual design, movement, sound. In any design process, know the rules so that you know when you can break them and how to break them effectively.

The people who originally put flat roofs on buildings as part of the modern movement ignored the fact that some slant to a roof had a useful function: shedding water. A lot of those buildings leaked badly. If they'd only asked themselves, "How do I avoid using a slanted roof, but still shed water?" Anticipate the problems when you're designing. That's the design challenge.

A1
Satin Brush Aluminum
2' x 8' x 1/4"

A2
Satin Brush Aluminum
2' x 6' x 1/4"

A3
Satin Brush Aluminum
2' x 4' x 1/4"

A4
Satin Brush Aluminum
2' x 2' x 1/4"

← As part of the planning for the Athletic Hall of Fame at Brigham Young University, this diagram by Infinite Scale Design Group maps out how information would be applied to the different sizes and locations of the exhibit signage. This included testing for the best sight lines.
Infinite Scale Design Group

Testing Isn't Make-work. The best approach is to stop thinking of testing as an extra option, and present it as a necessary, integrated part of the process, one that will help you and the client ensure that the project is successful for the client's audience.

Testing and Politics. "Testing takes some of the politics out of the decision-making process during projects," explains Kathryn Campbell of What's Next Interactive. Is there a sacred cow? Something that you think isn't a good idea, that perhaps the client insists on integrating into the project despite your protests? Don't argue, test! Is there an innovative solution you'd like to try, something that you think will be helpful for users that perhaps goes against what has come to be considered standard practice? Don't guess and don't think you have to design based on the strictest rules; you can test your ideas. The results may surprise you.

"Make everything as simple as possible, but not simpler."

—Albert Einstein

Qualitative data gained from testing prototypes can be particularly useful in validating concepts. These typical users evaluated possible approaches to simplifying the design of parking signage in New York City. Research has shown that ten participants reviewing prototypes can uncover 80 percent of the problems with a design approach. (See case study on page 132.)
Addison

"The world in which we live has become a cultural smorgasbord, and we all live permanently on the verge of indigestion. We have to have some help in sifting through the endless choices."

—Joe Jackson, Musician

THE TESTING PRACTICE

Make It Standard Practice. The best approach is to build testing into your project plan from the very beginning. Clients are likely to be more receptive if you explain that testing is simply part of your regular production process.

Test Iteratively. Test early and often. Iterative testing means you don't wait to test until you've spent weeks or months on the project. At project inception, find a selection of representative users and set up a regular testing schedule. Set aside a couple of hours each week for a simple informal test. Don't try to test everything at once. With dense information, there are often too many elements that you're still in the process of trying to figure out. Test individual segments of your design. Test whatever is ready at the time. If you're working on a website, test just the navigation titles one week. The next week test a set of icons. The next week you could test just the on/off states of the buttons, and so on.

PROTOTYPES AND TESTING TOOLS

Simple Paper Prototypes. Testing tools don't have to be fancy. Especially during the early stages in the project, test with paper prototypes. You don't need to videotape the test (although if you have the resources, you can). The most important thing is to get user feedback during the design process. Take good notes and/or perhaps record audio to catalog their responses. Have the design team spend time discussing the feedback. Then make some decisions on how the feedback will impact the next iteration of the design.

Advanced Prototypes. Once you've mapped out a good portion of the user experience of the information design, you can conduct more elaborate testing. If you're testing a website, you might test an entire path leading from the home page to subpages and a particular interactive tool. Even during advanced testing with interactive "clickable" prototypes, it's best to keep things relatively simple for each user-testing scenario by testing one path or one piece of functionality at a time.

How Finished Should Your Prototypes Be?
Testing a prototype that is still in a very abstract stage of design (for instance, website wireframes without any design elements) can be a real challenge for end users. "Those of us who have ended up in design careers," says Campbell, "tend to vastly overestimate how conceptual most people are. Most people are, cognitively, fairly literal. It doesn't mean they're unintelligent. Think about how hard it

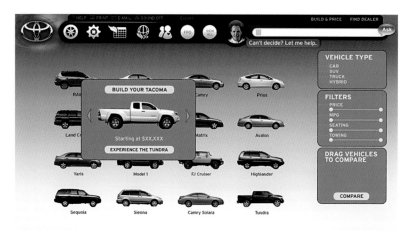

Several clickable prototypes of Toyota.com's car model selection tool were tested. In an early prototype, users didn't understand that the filters were slider bars and attempted to click on the circular end points as if they were buttons. Most users were overwhelmed by the filters, sort tools, and comparison tools that were grouped into one area. Several users bypassed the tools entirely without trying to figure out how to use them. In a later version, introductory copy and a change in design made the filter's slider bars more intuitive. Users also found the tool easier to explore and understand once the different functions were more clearly differentiated from each other. **What's Next Interactive Inc.**

is to convey to the client that a wireframe isn't really design. You have to make things look like the real thing or people get confused."

However, if you're in the early stages of a project at a point where most design issues have not been resolved and you decide to create a prototype that looks very "finished," you run the risk of testers, clients, and even designers confusing your testing materials with actual methodical, strategic visual design. People can get attached to the look that was quickly thrown together for the sake of a test. Plus, when something

looks like it could be the final design, you run the risk of having clients and users focus and give feedback on the visual elements you're not even testing, instead of on the information design issues for which you need feedback.

Bottom line: Make your testing prototypes look enough like the final product so it's clear to users that it's a website or even a subway map. Just don't spend so much time on making the testing prototype look so complete as an artifact that users mistake it for a design that is further along in the process than it actually is.

Campbell says, "I like to have the very last prototype that I test look darn final. But that's the very last test."

HOW TO FIND TESTERS

First, you'll need to know your main audience types. (See "Wrangling Audience and Content" in Chapter 2 for more information about determining audience types.)

Typically, your client should be able to provide you with a list of customers or appropriate users from their database. You can also get help gathering your test subjects by hiring a recruiting agency. These agencies contact potential testers, offer incentives, and even set up the test in a testing lab.

 A London-based information design firm regularly conducts customer and stakeholder research to determine best practices for simplifying invoices, bills, and forms. The goal is to increase customer satisfaction. This before-and-after example shows improvements made on a document for Sainsbury's Bank. **Boag Associates Ltd.**

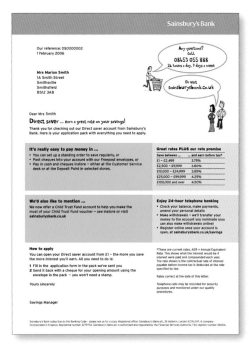

wildwood
school

In order to test the best direction for the look and feel for online and print applications, KBDA will often create mood boards to help the client visualize their options. To get input from geographically dispersed constituents, KBDA will often test an online presentation linked to a simple and inexpensive online survey application that can capture both quantitative and qualitative responses. **KBDA**

How Many Testers Do You Need? For the Allergan pharmaceuticals site, What's Next Interactive tested a site on three specific user types identified as the most important in terms of site traffic: doctors, patients, and Job seekers. How many users participated in the testing? Approximately six people from each user group. "Because of my background in traditional market research, I wasn't poised to believe this," says Campbell. "But you really only need to test your design on a few people. After about six interviews with a particular set of users, you find out about all the big issues for that user type."

SURVEYS VS. LIVE USER TESTING

When you want to test your design but don't have access to live testers or want a broader range of opinions, a survey may be an effective course. There are some basic tools that help you create and distribute surveys online. Or you can keep it really simple and email PDF or jpeg images of alternative designs to a wide sampling of users, asking for their preference.

On the other hand, if you want to know something specific, such as which button users will most likely push, which information they see as most important, or whether they understand a set of icons, it's probably best to test one-on-one with a smaller sampling of representative users.

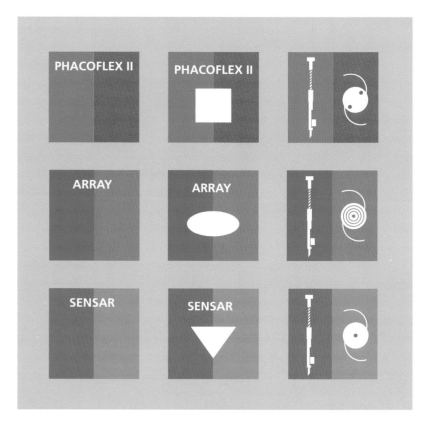

⬆ When Allergan asked KBDA to create new packaging for its line of intraocular lenses, research showed effective information design could help differentiate their products. The surgical nursing staff was hard-pressed to identify correct lens types in their high-stress, low-lit operating room environment. The stakes were high because the appropriate choice of lenses was crucial to the patient's recovery. Approaches were carefully tested with users. It was determined that using a combination of color-coding and graphic icons produced the most reliable results. **KBDA**

"You can only understand something new relative to something you already understand, whether visually, verbally, or numerically." —Richard Saul Wurman

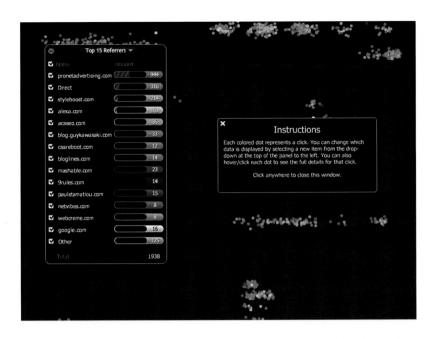

Crazy Egg creates data visualization software that helps people visually understand and analyze visitor traffic on their websites. This Confetti visualization shows a Flash visualization of all site clicks. The visualization lets you isolate the data you want to compare and hide the rest.
Crazy Egg, Inc.

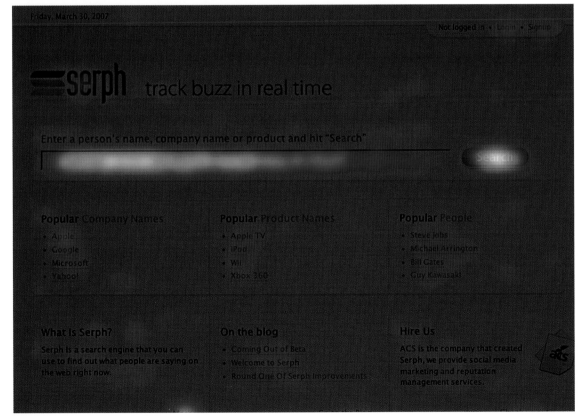

Crazy Egg's popular heatmap visualization provides a simple way for website owners to view the frequency of user clicks on particular parts of a site page. This allows for simple and fast analysis and decision-making regarding success of features and content on a site.
Crazy Egg, Inc.

Types of User Research and Testing

Different types of testing can occur during all project phases. At times, you'll want to employ all testing types in a project. Sometimes you'll need one or two types of testing, depending on project needs. Jeff Harris, founding partner and executive experience director at Atlanta-based Matter, outlines the various tests. Harris has a deep background in human-centered design and a range of experience in researching and testing design projects.

"There are some people who come into graphic design and find it a bit ephemeral and vacuous. People who like to do useful things are attracted to information design. There is something quite useful about designing traffic signs so people don't get lost or medicine bottles that people can understand. It's a way of making a difference. It's public service."

—David Sless

CONCEPT TESTS

Concept tests occur early in the project. Prototypes are simple and may not even have physical form. You present and get feedback on an idea. Instead of polling fellow designers with a concept test, you ask potential users about your design. You literally talk to someone about your idea.

You could be considering creating an online shopping site. With a concept test, you ask whether or not someone would be interested in buying your products online. The conversation is a "low-fidelity" sort of testing prototype.

You can do concept tests for any kind of design. For a museum experience, you might ask potential visitors what a museum visit should be like just using adjectives. Is the museum quiet or moody, fun or energetic?

PARTICIPATORY DESIGN

With participatory design, people use design exercises to sort through ideas. The participants will often do something during the test that will surprise you. This method works best when you interact one-on-one with the participant. You could use a card-sorting method to test how participants organize information. You might put content headers on cards or even Post-it notes and have the participants sort and group them by subject matter. Next, ask them to group the headers into categories. Essentially, your participants can create a website information architecture.

Use the card-sorting exercise for anything where you need to organize heaps of information: chapters in a book, a series of posters, or a museum layout.

DESIGN TESTING

Design testing occurs when you've finished concept exploration and you've decided on one concept for design development.

Just to rewind: Initial research allows you to become a proxy for your end users. If your client didn't pay for research, you're guessing what users want, making the best decisions you can. The purpose of design testing is to help you make decisions you don't feel comfortable making alone.

Working with testers individually is best. Show each participant how the poster, museum exhibit, or website might look and function and ask for feedback.

With design testing, there are different levels of prototype fidelity. For Web or software interfaces, you can show people mock-up wireframes in a PDF file or basic HTML. In packaging development, you build a model of the package. When you show your prototype to users, have them run through scenarios, or just ask them what they think. For print or packaging design, you may ask: "Can you read this? Is the type too small?" For interactive design testing, you look for feedback on interface behaviors and functionality. No question is too big or small. You can test a specific piece or the whole design.

FOCUS GROUPS

Traditional focus groups collect people from the same demographic to evaluate a fully developed product. Movie preview screenings are a common example of a focus group. Often, focus groups are conducted in an artificial environment—a lab or a room with a big mirror and people behind it.

The challenge with focus groups is "groupthink." Sometimes people hesitate to agree, or dominant personalities lead the conversation. You're usually putting strangers together, asking them to deal with social dynamics. People are afraid of saying something different from the crowd.

It's hard to get a group to engage with specific aspects of your design. Do you hand something out to everyone or pass something around and ask them to respond? Talk to the same people individually and you'll likely get their true opinion.

Focus groups work when groupthink is important. For quick consensus, a focus group can be useful. Focus groups also work when people aren't strangers: for example, groups who have the exact same job. When groups have common experience, social dynamics are reduced.

USABILITY TESTING

Usability testing reveals whether everything in the design is working. Is it intuitive? How steep is the learning curve? If I release it into the wild, will people figure it out?

We all take for granted certain social systems. Say an alien lands on Earth in a densely populated area. He enters what he thinks is a domicile and is confronted with somebody who directs him to a place to sit and hands him a manuscript, then

disappears. Another person comes by and offers him a liquid, then waits for him to do something. That's a restaurant. Socially, we all know how that system works: the maitre d', the table, the menu, and the waiter with a glass of water. To an alien, it's unknown and confusing.

A usability test ensures you haven't made so many assumptions with the design that people won't figure it out. Conduct tests all along the way and you may short-circuit many problems. Usability testing ensures that the work functions as designed—be it the readability of a poster, the navigation of a shopping center, or the effectiveness of hospital signage.

Time spent on a task is a key point in a usability test. You, as a project expert, can figure it out in five seconds, while a novice might take three minutes. Usability testing fine-tunes the solution before you go live.

BETA TESTING AND PERFORMANCE TESTING

Beta testers with interactive projects are looking for bugs in the code and doing performance testing for software. You can apply that same thinking to a museum experience. What if 50,000 people show up on opening day? How would the exhibit design handle that load?

Once you've settled on a concept, design testing with paper prototypes can ensure that you incorporate user feedback into your process.
Matter

You can have users participate in the initial design planning process by having them help you organize your project content. Using simple Post-it notes, testers can sort content into the categories that make the most sense to them.
Matter

"If you ever find yourself designing something a certain way because *you* think it would be better that way, then you're probably performing art and not design. Art is about self-expression. Design is selfless."

—Jeff Harris, Matter

All the key principles of good design apply when it comes to information design projects, whether they're print, environmental, or interactive. Some of the basic tools that designers have been trained to use are particularly effective in solving information design challenges.

The following sections explore the ways designers have used devices like color, structure, scale, and rhythm, as well as motion and sound, to develop powerful information design solutions.

DESIGN TOOLKIT

4

- → Color
- → Type Styling
- → Weight and Scale
- → Structure
- → Grouping
- → Graphic Elements
- → Imagery
- → Sound and Motion

Color

An extremely important tool for an information designer, color is a very effective way to convey differentiation. (Remember when you first learned a red light means stop, and a green one means go?) Color can also provide a sense of wayfinding, allowing readers to scan text and quickly isolate elements such as subheads and bullets.

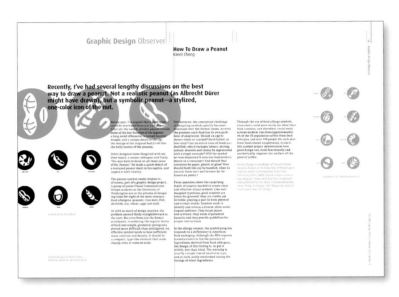

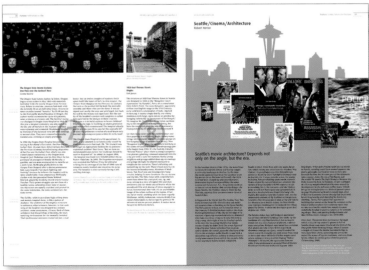

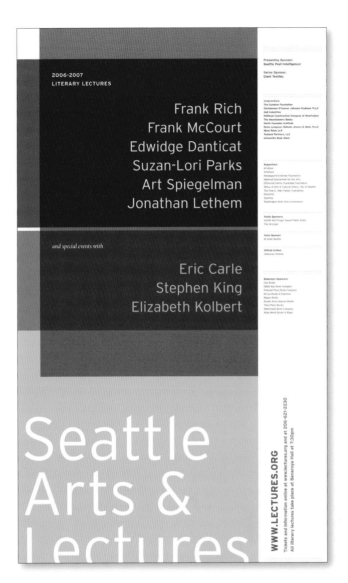

Arcade, a design and architecture publication based in the northwestern U.S., uses a single bold accent color each issue, integrating it into type styling, graphic illustrations, and wayfinding devices.
Push Design

Clear hierarchies are established by using different fields of color to contain different types of content in this poster for a lecture series.
Cheng Design

> "Hierarchical variables can be expressed by means of size and intensity, and distinguishing variables by means of color and form." —Paul Mijksenaar

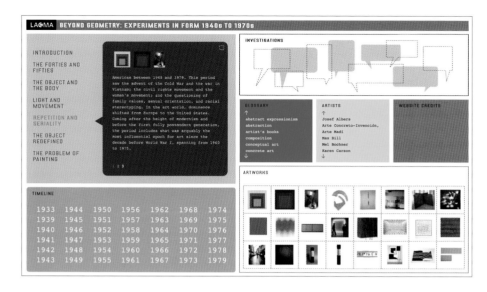

Crosby Associates designed the template for *Communiqué,* the email newsletter for AIGA, using a simple two-color palette. Employing only one HTML typeface, the red accent color allows the reader to quickly scan the "table of contents" of jump links at the top, and to easily navigate through the subheads for the subsequent articles.
AIGA

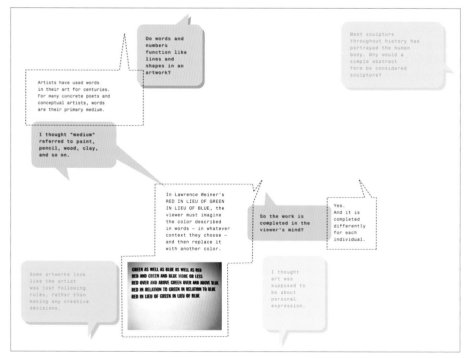

In this website for a museum exhibit, bold color contains and highlights the content for easy navigation.
Louise Sandhaus Design/ Durfee Regn Sandhaus

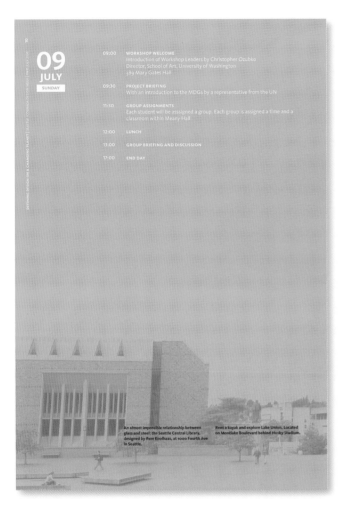

This system of conference materials (above and right) effectively employs color coding to categorize program sections and the schedule of events for different types of conference attendees.
Push Design

Type Styling

The styling of type is another key way to differentiate types of information and establish a sense of hierarchy. You might highlight one or two type elements in a simple invitation—or work with a carefully chosen palette of typefaces to clarify varied types of content in a complex reference book or a financial report.

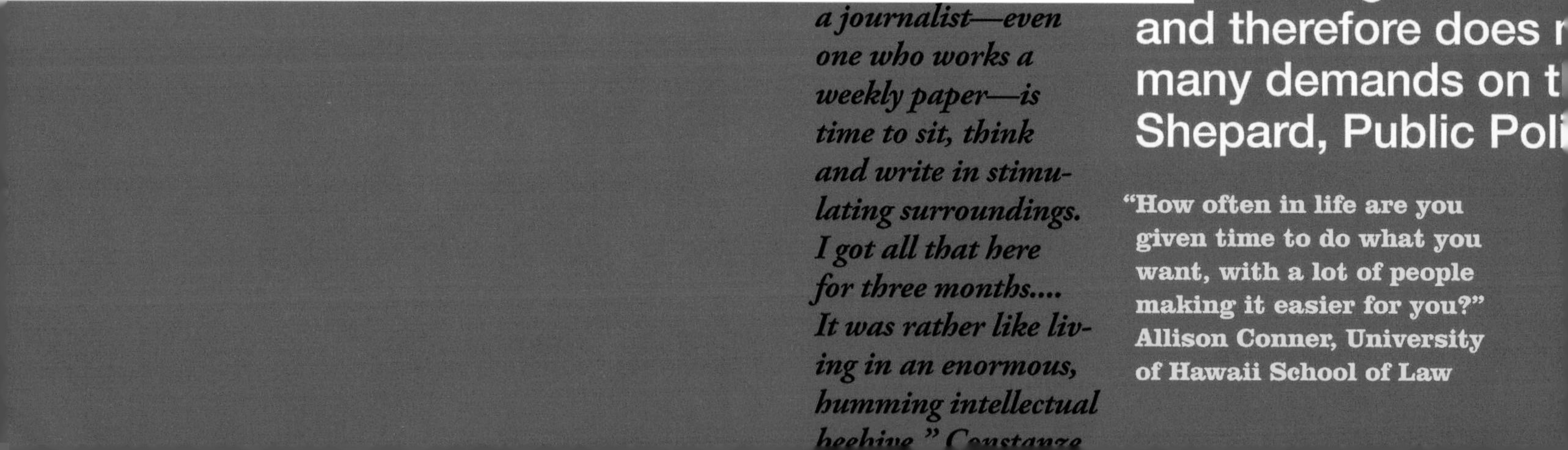

Vilson

ith about the
about the affair
nowledge and

as been great to
institution which
htly, that most of
working hard on
and therefore does
many demands on t
Shepard, Public Poli

a journalist—even one who works a weekly paper—is time to sit, think and write in stimulating surroundings. I got all that here for three months.... It was rather like living in an enormous, humming intellectual beehive." Constanze

"How often in life are you given time to do what you want, with a lot of people making it easier for you?" Allison Conner, University of Hawaii School of Law

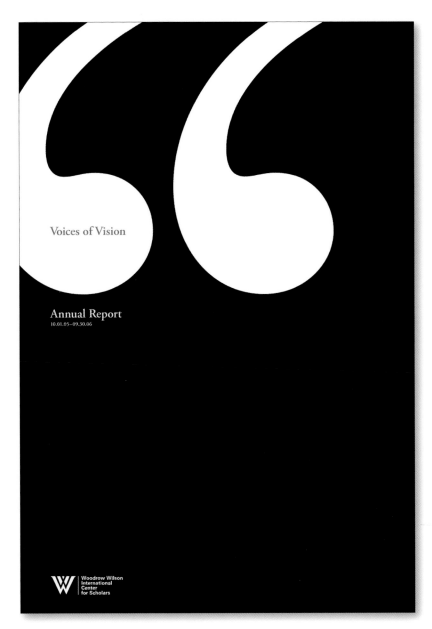

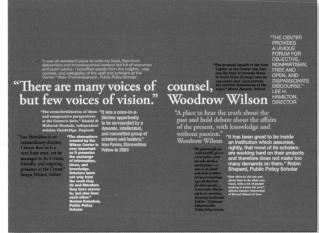

Complementary typefaces
in a variety of sizes and
weights accent content in an
effective and visually dynamic
way in this annual report for
the Woodrow Wilson Center.
Design Army

Type styling differentiates
several types of information
shown here in *Worldchanging*,
a book that reports on new,
positive developments in
science, engineering, architecture, business, and politics.
Sagmeister Inc.

"The function of the designer is to increase the legibility of the world." —Will Burtin

Bold pull quotes are strategically placed in this redesign of *Juxtapoz* magazine, featuring artwork by Seonna Hong.
Hybrid Design

Boldfaced content headers help readers quickly find what they need on a text-intensive home page for the Prostate Cancer Foundation website.
KBDA

Weight and Scale

As a way to read quickly, human beings scan patterns and differences. Changes in the weight and scale of artwork and typographic elements can signal that certain pieces of information have been prioritized. This technique can be used very effectively in combination with color and type styling to clarify complex hierarchies.

CONNE

Students and Fa
The Communit
People to Mater
Scholars Everyw

The U.Va. Library has
or connecting people
The future includes m
only in physical space
far beyond Charlotte
sharing knowledge is
effort, with increasing

Monarda Coccinea, or Scarlet R
from *The family flora and mater*
botanica ... by Peter P. Good, 1
in the "Garden in the Library" ex

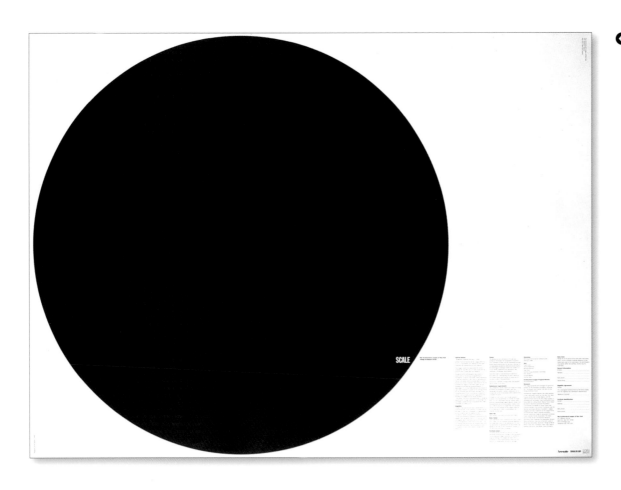

This poster announces the Architectural League of New York's annual competition for young architects, with the chosen theme of "scale." The title of the show appears in 35-point type in a 35-inch (88.9 cm)-diameter black dot.
Pentagram Design

Because of its scale and contrast, this factoid can be quickly absorbed by a "flip-through" reader. The oversized numeral attracts the eye and increases memorability.
Vanderbyl Design

Since 1970, total emissions of air pollutants have been reduced 25%

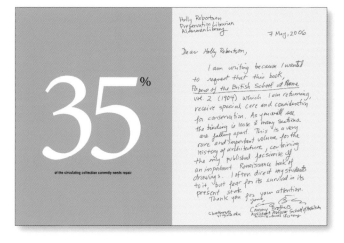

Large, capitalized type knocked out against a dark background communicates the most important information for this poster announcing the speaker lineup for an upcoming lecture series. Supporting text is smaller and contained in a separate part of the composition.
Cheng Design

Varied typography creates a rich visual language in these spreads from the Library of the University of Virginia's 2006 annual report.
Design Army

"Graphic design is a form of translation."

—Simon Johnston

← Weight and scale help to distinguish types of information in a series of museum posters. **Fauxpas Grafik**

→ This book's design is surprisingly varied despite the use of a single typeface. Weight and scale establish hierarchies. **thomas.matthews**

Structure

Bauhaus pioneers helped codify the use of the grid as a compelling communications tool. Carefully planned grids and white space can help a reader navigate through complex information. In addition, the very structure of the project—whether it's the physicality of a print piece, the pacing of a multimedia project, or the organization of an exhibit—can convey additional meaning.

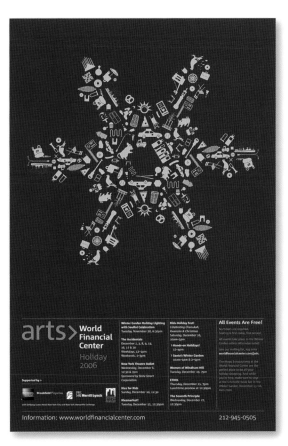

These foldout newsletters for the World Financial Center use a recurring structure to consistently accommodate different types of information for each issue of the publication. **Open**

This website's structure allows the client to update content easily without sacrificing the integrity of the original design. **KBDA**

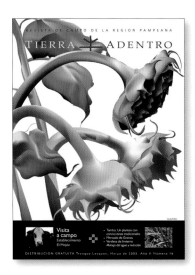

Magazine covers for *Tierra Adentro* use a consistent grid, ensuring that regular readers can find the information that is of most interest to them.
Guerrini Design Island

Structured, offset columns of type complement the organic black-and-white photo silhouettes in this annual report for the Sydney Dance Company. The placement of the silhouettes creates a sense of movement that helps the viewer navigate through the information. The numbering system encourages a sense of momentum.
Frost Design

→ A consistent but variable grid gives readers an easy-to-scan but fresh approach in this recurring feature on branded products in BMW's quarterly consumer magazine.
50,000feet, Inc.

← The *Urban Origami* book uses an unusual structure to communicate the architectural subject matter. The book encourages the reader to fold the paper in the book as a reference to the architect's fold motifs in the building.
Blank Mosseri

Grouping

Clustering information can help readers quickly locate the information they are seeking, whether it be in a simple poster or a complex multi-media project. Multiple entry points allow a reader to absorb information as visual sound bites. The grouping of information can also signal hierarchies of importance, particularly when used in conjunction with changes in color, weight, and scale.

Your car could warn you of traffi relay mechanical diagnostics back manufacturer. Your refrigerator cabinet could keep track of its co request a delivery when supplies home entertainment center could just-released song or video. And locate lost keys—or a lost pet—b to a global positioning system.

Sound far-fetched? Actually, mos technologies exist right now. All are the right kinds of communica Pervasive networking isn't scienc it's the next phase in the evolutic world infosphere.

"Every day the World Wide Web

roughly a million electronic pc

to the hundreds of millions alr

For the first time in history, m

people have virtually instant c

their homes and offices to the

output of a significant—and

fraction of the planet's popul

Age

Network access required.

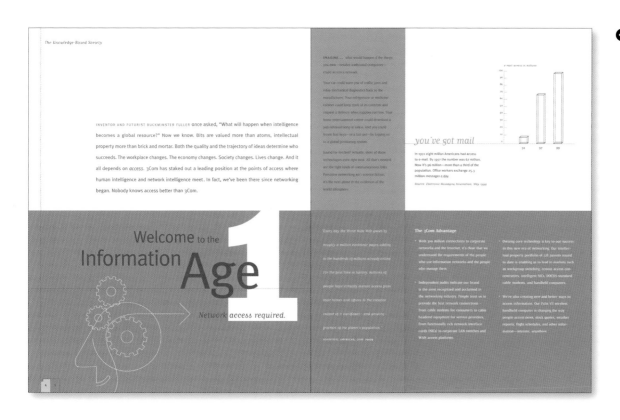

Color fields contain different types of content in this annual report for a U.S.-based technology company. Each spread focuses on a key market trend, expressed through "sound bites" such as charts, testimonials, and bulleted strategy statements. Each content type is identified by typographic shifts in size, weight, and style.
KBDA

These quarterly newsletters cluster information in a consistent way to maximize readability and coherence despite a great deal of content in a limited amount of space.
Axis41

Sidebars help to identify content related to the main story elements in this magazine for UCLA.
KBDA

An elegant grid helps to organize types of information in this website for a German architecture office.
Fauxpas Grafik

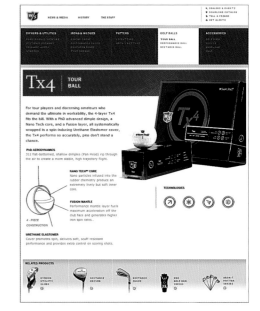

The pages of Wilson Staff's consumer website are organized into several different areas to accommodate visitors with different levels of interest in and knowledge about the featured golf products. (See case study on page 184.)
VSA Partners

modern organic products

mop extreme moisture

treatment for dry hair

hydratant extrême crème de soin pour cheveux secs

Anyone who washes their hair daily, goes out in the sun, styles with heat or chemically treats will benefit from this protective, moisture replenishing treatment. Contains Certified Organic Banana Apple Juice & other good stuff.

6.76 fl oz / 200 mL

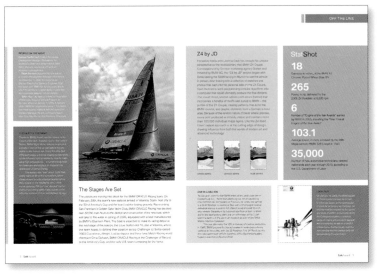

"Changes in the visual organization of a document can lead to changes in how people perceive its content."

—Karen A. Schriver

Graphic Elements

The intricately adorned initial caps found in medieval manuscripts are early examples of the ways graphic artists have always employed graphic elements to help readers navigate through content. Lines, rules, bullets, and other devices are tools designers still use to purposefully attract the eye. These devices can also provide direction and punctuation.

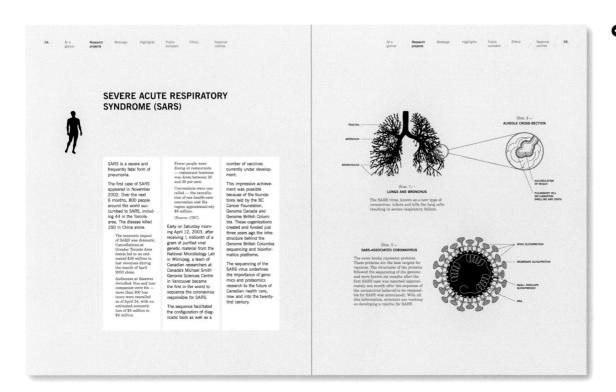

This prototype for a washer/dryer interface employs simple icons and graphics to make the interface easy to understand.
K.J. Chun

"The ability to find something goes hand-in-hand with how well it's organized."

—Richard Saul Wurman

Despite the complexity, an elegant sense of balance and careful attention to detail create visual interest and coherence in this two-page ad.
50,000feet, Inc.

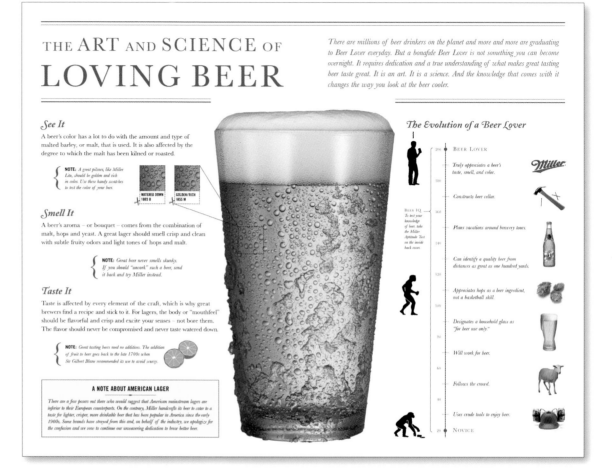

Graphic shapes draw attention to messages on this website for Strathmore Papers.
VSA Partners

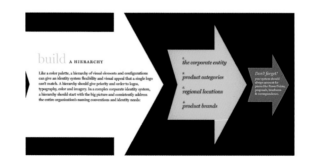

Graphic icons and a categorized legend illustrate the distribution of Dutch aid resources in Afghanistan in this spread from the magazine *Vrij Nederland*.
Information Design Studio

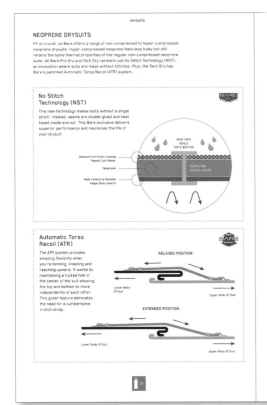

Keyline boxes sort complex technical information in this BARE catalog of diving products.
Rethink

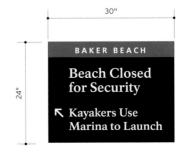

Graphic elements such as rules and scale drawings help to organize detailed instructions for signage in Golden Gate Park. (See case study on page 200.)
Hunt Design

Imagery

Reader studies show that the marriage of text and image is one of the most powerful ways to help a reader retain information. Publications know a "flip through" reader may not read paragraphs of text, but will very likely read a caption for an intriguing image. Designers can also help distill information by creating effective graphics.

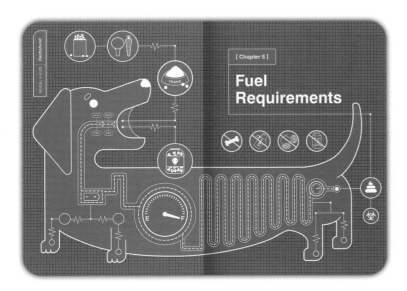

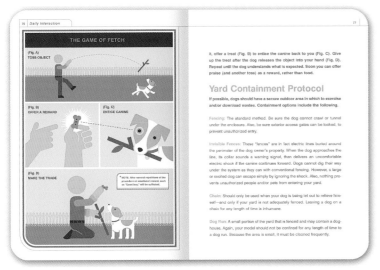

Playful illustrations, diagrams, and icons give dog lovers access to information in this humorous adaptation of the familiar owners' manual.
Headcase Design

Key messages are seamlessly integrated into the photographic background, as well as splattered in the foreground of this poster.
Harmen Liemburg

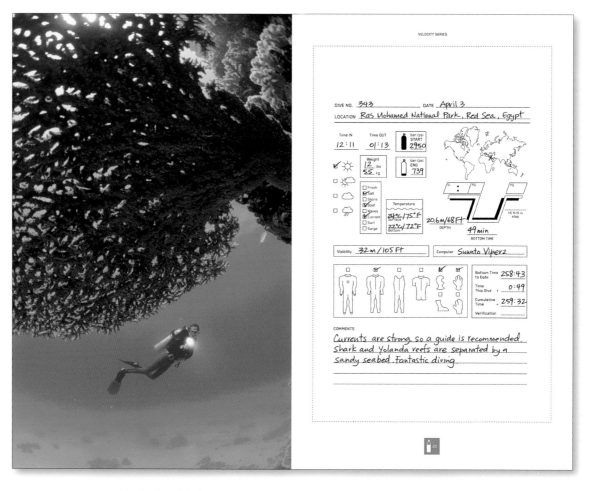

➡ Deep-sea photographs provide an evocative counterpart to the technical information arrayed on the right side of these catalog spreads for BARE wetsuits. **Rethink**

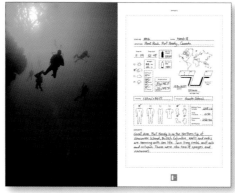

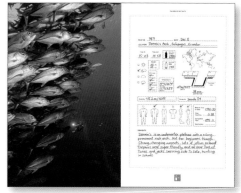

"Information design is clear thinking made visible."

—William Lutz

Simple, bold photographs and headlines draw visitors to approach these environmental graphics. Once there, they discover and read more detail.
Landesberg Design

Martin Lipman's quirky photography of folded paper illustrates the key themes of this annual report for the Forest Products Association of Canada.
McMillan

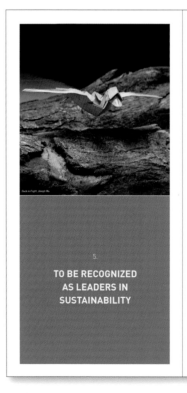

Sound and Motion

Interactive media provides two additional tools—sound and motion. Research has consistently shown that many people absorb information more aurally, while others rely more on visual cues. Combining sound with graphic devices can have a powerful effect. Motion draws an audience's attention and creates a sense of narrative that leaves a memorable impression.

This promotional website for IKEA simulates a 360-degree view that users can manipulate to see furniture products in a virtual home environment.
Forsman & Bodenfors

The website for UK design firm johnson banks incorporates motion into its playful site navigation. Users drill down to magnify items of specific interest without ever losing their way. A miniature graphic of the home page's content is ever-present on-screen as a reference point.
johnson banks

On returning to johnsonbanks.co.uk you'll see it merrily attempts to say what we do In a nutshell, Answer your questions, show you our latest work for The Beatles and a cross-section of Recent projects. You can still Contact us here. But we know that if we're going to blag a spot in your bookmarks menu you'll need something worth returning to. Some problems solved starts generic then gets specific whilst the word-shy amongst you could Climb the work tree. You might want to See some pictures or only want Words. You can Download stuff or even go Shopping. Honest. There's still a Thought for the week, updated weekly. We're amazed we have the Time.

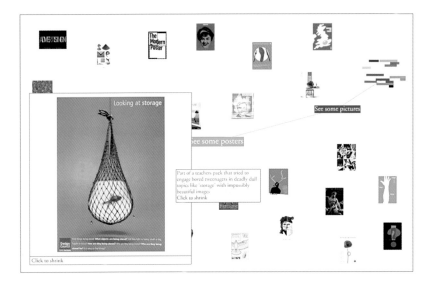

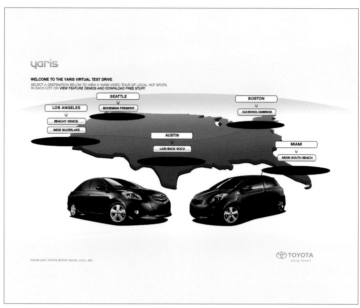

The Toyota Yaris sitelet incorporates animated features that
encourage visitors to click through
to learn more about the vehicle.
Users can also select different
points of view on the virtual test-
drive feature, to simulate the
experience of driving in the car.
Saatchi & Saatchi

Nine LCD screens in the lobby of New York's Museum of Modern Art (MoMA) display a continuous motion-graphics installation that provides visitors with information to help them plan their visit. The piece simultaneously highlights the range, diversity, and quality of the museum's collection. The colorful "panoramic barcode" transitions help to fuse the dialog between information, art, and entertainment for visitors waiting in line. (Photography provided by FCharles Photography.)
Imaginary Forces

This diagram illustrates how animated slivers of more than 20,000 works of art from MoMA's database can be layered with images related to events, exhibitions, and other promotions to juxtapose information, art, and retail in a cohesive mix.
Imaginary Forces

Charles & Ray Eames:
A Retrospective

Special Exhibitions, 3 Floor

Through January 31

IMAGE
CONTEXT
PROCESS
IMAGE BLUR
FINGERPRINT
HEADINGS
LOCATION
DATES

The need for effective information design spans every medium, and includes print, interactive, packaging, and environmental projects. The following case studies represent some of the most accomplished work being done in the field today.

Whether you're perusing a magazine, reading a manual for a new piece of equipment, or looking at product packaging in a store, words are ubiquitous. With so much printed matter around us, sometimes it's difficult to separate the useful information from the extraneous. The most successful information design in print entices people to read and clearly communicates key messages.

PRINTED MATTER
CASE STUDIES

5

→ **Carbone Smolan Agency**

→ **Smart Design**

→ **Addison**

→ **Pentagram Design**

→ **And Partners**

→ **Simon & Goetz Design**

Intellectual Capital

Case Study
Morgan Stanley

Project
Graphic Standards

Design Firm
Carbone Smolan Agency

For years, the financial services sector lagged behind others in employing design as a strategic tool. Facing an increasingly competitive marketplace, Morgan Stanley realized that design initiatives could address key business challenges. With over 600 offices in thirty-one countries, information is the essential currency Morgan Stanley shares with its global clients.

The company wanted to move beyond materials that were, at best, straightforward and understated. Their materials needed to project a more progressive approach, with engaging content that would increase their customers' perception of Morgan Stanley's added value. The company also wanted to streamline workflow processes and production costs.

Carbone Smolan created a comprehensive three-tiered system for all of Morgan Stanley's corporate events.

Finding the Right Partner. Morgan Stanley understood it was in the business of financial services, not graphic design, so it engaged the New York City-based design firm Carbone Smolan Agency (CSA) as a strategic partner.

The Daily Bash. CSA was initially hired to address a couple of long-standing dilemmas. To share information with key clients around the world, Morgan Stanley produces at least 300 events a year. Noting a lack of consistency in its event materials and inefficiencies in the internal processes required to produce each event, Morgan Stanley asked CSA to develop a series of recommendations.

After carefully reviewing the challenges, CSA helped the company develop a three-tiered architecture for its calendar of events, with detailed graphic standards for each event type. Collaborating with Morgan Stanley's writers, CSA developed clear informational hierarchies for everything from invitations to signage and programs, allowing Morgan Stanley to consistently convey key messages.

To streamline communication and create good internal ambassadors for the program, some of Morgan Stanley's in-house design staff worked in CSA's offices as the guidelines were in development. Once the guidelines were implemented globally, internal feedback was solicited from Morgan Stanley's offices around the world and CSA made "tweaks" to the document. Cultures as diverse as Asia, Japan, Europe, and North America embraced the system with a 99 percent rate of adoption worldwide.

MORGAN STANLEY LINE OF BUSINESS

Unseemly Flood of Data. Morgan Stanley then asked CSA to attack a "whole other kettle of fish"—the process by which the company published its in-depth research reports. Written by research analysts worldwide and distributed to clients, these reports lacked consistency.

In its initial research for the project, it was discovered that typical users received these reports each morning via email. Because clients typically received 300–400 messages every morning—including reports from competitor firms—it was imperative to help the reader quickly sort through the deluge. In a "survival of the fittest" play, CSA recommended that something as simple as changing the email slug line could offer a strategic advantage.

But even if the message was opened, a 20- to -100 page attachment could cause the reader to close it—or worse, delete it— with nary a look back. The antidote? CSA developed a sophisticated information hierarchy for the first page of each report, with standards for how headlines and initial text needed to be written and typeset. Putting the analyst's conclusions front and center allowed readers to "cut to the chase," and then allowed readers, if so inclined, to drill down to more detail in subsequent pages. The template allowed the reader to quickly and consistently identify the most important information.

Based on this strategic approach to information design, CSA was subsequently asked to work on Morgan Stanley's overall graphic standards, tackling enterprise-wide issues.

(back)

Save–the–date (front)

Invitation and Envelope

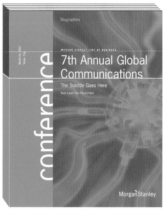

Program

Biography Book

Freestanding Banner

The materials for each event category were defined by a unified design approach.

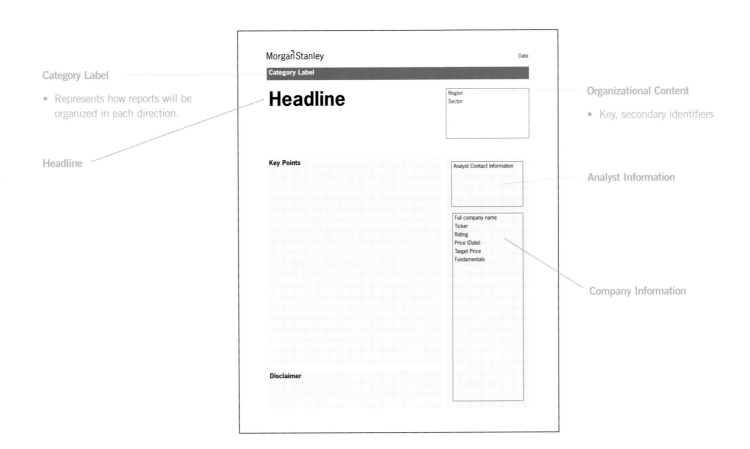

Category Label

- Represents how reports will be organized in each direction.

Headline

Organizational Content

- Key, secondary identifiers

Analyst Information

Company Information

In order to help Morgan Stanley organize, categorize, and effectively deliver its Equity Research reports, CSA developed schematic layouts to test and analyze relevant content.

Detailed design standards reinforce a judicious use of copy editing to present pertinent information in a clear, concise fashion.

Showcasing a Better Mousetrap

Case Study
simplehuman

Project
Packaging

Design Firm
Smart Design

Founded by an entrepreneurial CEO who figured out how to "build a better mousetrap," simplehuman, a home product design company, created an elegant, well-engineered, yet affordable trash can that appealed to people with contemporary taste. It was especially timely given a trend toward commercial-grade kitchens in the home, complete with well-designed, high-performance appliances.

When simplehuman needed to develop a logo and a packaging language, they chose Smart Design because the firm knew the "space" well, having done similar work for OXO, another company specializing in high-end housewares.

As a contrast to the clean white backgrounds and the neutral colors in the product photography, a clean, vibrant color palette was developed to attract attention.

Performance Driven. With a focus on consumer products, Smart Design's packaging and branding efforts are informed by years of design experience. The designers understand that, just like the product itself, packaging needs to meet performance objectives. With little control over how the product would be displayed in large retail environments chock-full of competing products, they needed to create packaging that would stand out from the clutter. As Smart Design cofounder Tom Dair says, "Most retail packaging is overly complex and gimmicky. We knew we could make the packaging stand out by paring back the imagery and text to the essential elements."

Since most retail environments are self-serve, the packaging had to attract and educate. This was particularly important given that simplehuman didn't have a big budget for print or broadcast advertising. The packaging was both the billboard and the sales representative.

Knowing consumers are time-stressed and hassled about making purchasing decisions, the goal was to have the package highlight the product's areas of innovation. Smart Design was careful to use benefit statements rather than listing features. Dair says, "If you focus on product features, you're leaving it up to the consumer to figure out how the features become beneficial."

placement

the choice of material is best suited for the different functional needs in each room

metal step can

most versatile can - ideal for bathrooms and kitchens

plastic step can

durable and bright for kid's rooms or bathrooms

wood can

designed for a study or library – with a plastic inner liner

sure-fit liners

designed specifically for SimpleHuman cans

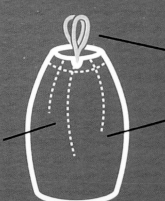

pull-tight handles for easy disposal

thick, high quality plastic for durable, worry free use

designed to fit our cans perfectly for clean and easy use

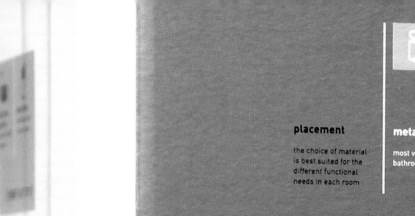

simplehuman™

tools for efficient living

simplehuman™

tools for efficient living

IamSteel

butterfly step can

"**Good design, good typography is a function of information and inspiration, of the conscious and unconscious, of yesterday and today, of fact and fantasy, work and play, craft and art.**" —Paul Rand

Some products sold at higher price points, so it was important to differentiate the product from competitors to help the consumer clarify the different features/benefits in the simplehuman line.

Modular System. In addition to cartons, the designers developed a system for detailed but elegant labels attached to the product itself, so customers could get information even if retailers took the products out of the boxes to save display space.

In addition to boxes, Smart Design developed a system for detailed but elegant labeling for the product itself, so customers could get information even if retailers took the products out of the boxes to save display space.

In order to convey a look that is sleek and modern but also simple and friendly, the front panel features a "hero shot" of the product with a simple overlay of elegant type. There was a heavy emphasis on white space to help it stand out in the cluttered retail environments.

Because simplehuman was committed to developing additional product lines, it was important to create a modular approach to the visual language. The design had to be unified but flexible, and work for accessories as well.

Success has meant that simplehuman's in-house design department continues to implement the system. The product line looks cohesive, even with packaging that's quite different in terms of size, shape, and materials.

As Dair says, "You're helping to set the consumer's expectation. Luckily, these are great products. We didn't have to create a lot of vapor around them. We just needed to reflect the company's commitment to creating tools for efficient living."

↑ Simple line drawings draw attention to bulleted lists so consumers can review product benefits at a glance.

← The product line looks cohesive —even with packaging that is quite different in terms of size, shape, and materials.

Simplified Global Communications

Case Study
Various

Project
Various

Design Firm
Addison

When Gordon Akwera joined Addison, a creative services company in New York City that specializes in strategic business communications, he became part of a start-up practice known as simplified communications. The goal was to simplify the complex marketing and customer communications for Addison's global clients.

Prior to joining Addison, Akwera's experience included creating information graphics for major mainstream periodicals. He had also worked for a firm that specialized in information design for high-stakes intellectual property law cases, and was trained to find ways to clearly convey complex ideas. As he notes, "Once you've learned to convey how complex, innovative inventions—such as genetic DNA engineering—work, you can clarify almost anything."

> **"It's important to accept we don't have all the right answers. In my view, the information designer is a facilitator. The key is to ask the right questions, observe, and process the cues."**
>
> —Gordon Akwera

The Right Time for Simplification.
At Addison, the time was right for taking the simplification message to the corporate world. The Securities and Exchange Commission (SEC), which regulates all publicly traded companies in the U.S., was scrutinizing companies that weren't adequately disclosing the details of their businesses to investors. Investing in better communications had become a hot button for Fortune 500 and midsize financial companies.

Systematic Approach. Since most business communications problems and deficiencies are mainly systematic, doing the job right entailed digging deep. In Akwera's first client assignment with Addison, it became clear he needed to examine communications at every customer touch point.

Addison quickly realized it wasn't enough to make recommendations about plain English writing and design. They needed to spend time with the internal departments to understand how the pieces were being produced. They had to look at each company's communications ecology. "If the systems weren't addressed, real change wouldn't occur," explains Akwera.

The Customer *Really* Matters. As time went on, Addison realized how critical it was to address these communications systems from a user-centric point of view.

→ Addison helped Merrill Lynch develop a modular content management system to streamline thousands of overlapping letters and notices. This program reduced operational burdens and costs, and enhanced customer satisfaction.

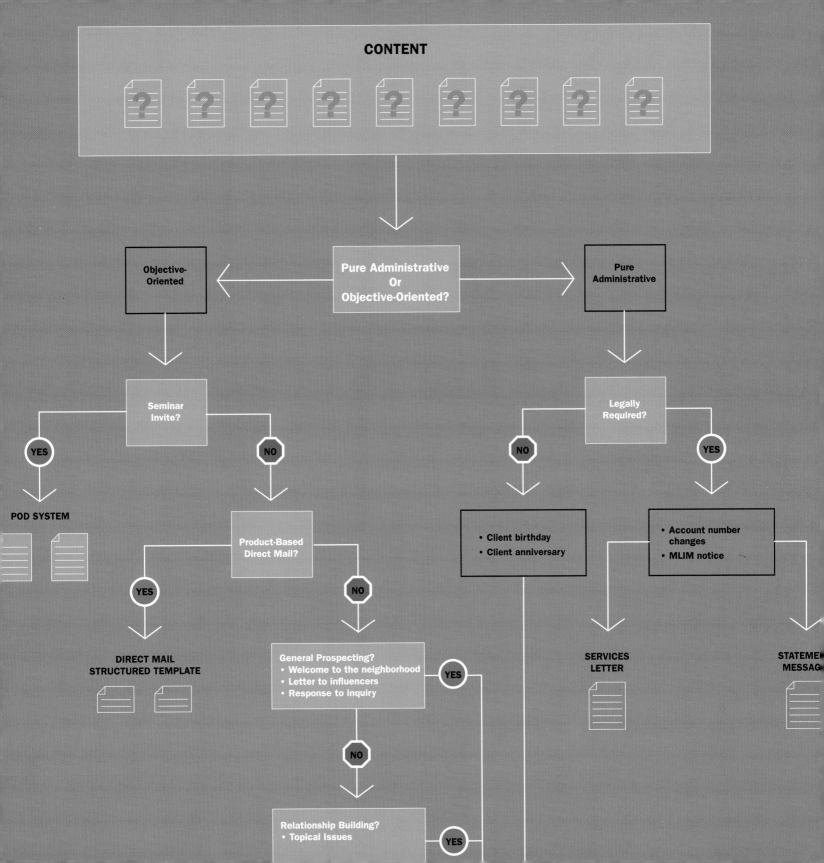

↑ Dense text with long, complex sentences and a hard-to-read format made this financial report for Xerox difficult to understand.

→ Addison created much more impact by highlighting key information with bold, clear graphics. Descriptions were all written in plain English and text was styled for easier reading.

→ Addison worked with Wells Fargo to simplify its suite of materials targeted to consumers. Accessible online, these product fact sheets allow readers to very quickly find the information they need. Type styles and sidebars provide clear information hierarchies.

Many companies create communications based on their internal workings. "It's product push. Come up with it, name it, make product collateral, and push your new product," says Akwera.

In contrast, Addison developed a discovery process through which they began spending time interviewing and observing their clients' customer interactions. They worked to identify the information customers required, and the types of problems customers really needed to solve. Addison now frequently conducts ethnographic research, spending time with customers in their day-to-day settings. They are able to observe differences between what people say they do and what actually takes place.

As a result of analyzing these interactions, Addison can point out where an organization's existing information is redundant, insufficient, or confusing. Addison provides analysis with an "outside-in" perspective. "Customers are saying, 'Give me the information I need, and in the most convenient way.' We help clients visualize how this can be done," says Akwera.

Fewer Trees, Happier Customers. The end result? In one case, over 5,000 communication pieces were effectively reduced to less than 100, resulting in significant cost savings and stakeholder satisfaction. Apart from elimination and consolidation, some of the information was moved to other channels such as online. Akwera says, "The money spent to give customers a better experience can result in years of return. After seeing metrics, companies come back and say, 'What else can you do for us?'"

When asked what it takes to be a good information designer, Akwera has two answers: "Patience and humility will lead you to the heart of the matter. It's important to accept that we don't have all the right answers. In my view, the information designer is a facilitator. The key is to ask the right questions, observe, and process the cues," he says.

"We're trying to help meet end user needs. Understanding their 'mental model' is fundamental. Once you nail it, there's always an 'aha' moment. Once you experience this insight, you realize you can apply research to every kind of communication challenge. It's eye opening," says Akwera.

↑ Extremely confusing parking signs posted throughout New York City result in millions of dollars in fines each year.

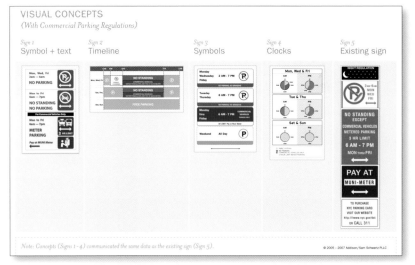

↑ As part of a pro bono project, Addison explored four preliminary design concepts for new parking signage. Addison tested these prototypes against the existing signage in order to determine what would be the most effective approach.

Reinventing an Icon

Case Study
TIME Magazine

Project
Magazine Redesign

Design Firm
Pentagram Design

When *TIME* magazine decided to reinvent itself, its longtime art director, Arthur Hochstein, enlisted an outside design firm to help meet the incredibly ambitious project target date. Hochstein hired four firms for the initial discovery phase, paying each firm to develop concepts from both a design and content perspective. The brief: Create a newsweekly that people would want to read. Because the Web is now often the medium of choice for breaking news, each firm understood that it was critical for the magazine to provide context and analysis. Hochstein notes, "There was no right answer. Each firm took a very different approach to the assignment." After much review, the Pentagram Design team, led by Paula Scher and Luke Hayman, was chosen for the job.

Even *TIME*'s venerable cover format was renewed. The logo was slightly reduced in scale, and a discreet set of typographic "billboards" was introduced to signal highlights for readers.

Addicted to Pubs? A transplanted Brit working in New York City, Hayman has spent more than 80 percent of his working life designing publications. "I keep trying to get out of it, but I keep getting sucked back in," he says. "I enjoy working on a range of projects, and I particularly love designing books, but I do like the ephemeral quality of magazines. It allows you to continuously keep trying things." Prior to the *TIME* assignment, Hayman had most recently been the art director at *New York Magazine* for almost three years.

The Grid Reigns Supreme. While Hayman is an avid experimenter, he's also an adamant champion of a strong, grid-based approach to publication design. He strongly believes in using a limited palette of fonts and color. "Flyers for secondhand suit stores are now full of color," he says, "so color doesn't have as much value as it used to. While designers might feel that a restrained type and color palette is restrictive or even boring, a reader often has only minutes to scan a publication. Consistent formatting can guide them through it, and separate the editorial pages from all the ads." He adds, "A pared-down palette allows the liveliness of the art to come through, so you can focus on great photo editing, illustration, and information graphics."

Illegal in America

While their future is bartered in the chambers of the Senate, illegal aliens continue to toil in the nation's fields and factories. Photographer SAMANTHA APPLETON shows their lives in the shadows and correspondent NATHAN THORNBURGH makes the case for amnesty. A TIME special report

"**With a strong grid and a consistent and defined approach to all the type, you give up a bit of spontaneity, but the magazine feels unified. It has the feeling of a beautifully proportioned building that's been built with a leveling tool.**" —Arthur Hochstein

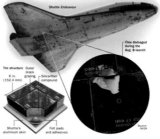

TIME's new managing editor, Rick Stengel, felt traditional news photography had been commoditized, and wanted to provide images that took a less literal approach. The emphasis is on finding images that provide a sense of storytelling.

The new design emphasized multiple access points for readers who might spend only moments scanning a story and avoid reading type set in continuous paragraphs.

The visual solutions needed to reflect the substantial changes being made in the editorial approach, so everything was in a state of flux. As Hochstein says, "The last thing we wanted was just a cosmetic change." Executing the project was so intensive that Hayman was "embedded" in *TIME*'s offices, working with the internal team for several months.

What Should Stay? What Should Go?

Hayman feels strongly that every redesign needs to begin with an exploration into the heritage of the publication's brand. "*TIME* is authoritative. It has decades of history to justify this positioning. We didn't want to make something trendy and cool. It needed to project a distinct point of view. It needed to say: These are serious times. We're smart. We're the place to go."

Instead of a continuous flow of stories, a three-part structure was developed for the reinvented magazine. Bold typography serves as a wayfinding and pacing device to signal the start of new sections, and provides a sense of rhythm. Each section has its own identity.

Early in the process Hayman recommended that *TIME* embrace Franklin Gothic as part of its design DNA. The typeface was a critical part of the redesign done in 1977 by renowned art director Walter Bernard. The bold setting provides a powerful punch—giving headlines additional "color," in contrast to text type.

Making the Technical Approachable

Case Study
Mohawk Fine Papers Inc.

Project
Brochures

Design Firm
And Partners

Mohawk Fine Papers Inc. is the largest premium paper manufacturer in North America. Mohawk's writing, text, cover, and digital papers include some of the best-known brands in the industry. The company has always been known for the quality of the promotional materials that they send to printers and designers all over the world. They are consistently well conceived and beautifully executed.

As part of its ongoing strategy to make promotions double as useful tools, the company looked at updating its website and online resource center. In addition, Mohawk moved to unify its core suite of promotional brochures, which addressed topics such as paper basics and sustainability.

Simple, elegant, geometric illustrations on the covers branded the series.

It's All About the User Experience.
Mohawk commissioned the New York City–based firm And Partners to build a suite of timeless reference tools that would be pertinent to junior designers, as well as those with far more experience. Used as printed "ambassadors" by Mohawk's sales reps, the brochures would encourage people to look for more detailed content on the Web.

Begin with Content. With this in mind, And Partners' founder, David Schimmel, decided to build the system "from the ground level." And Partners reviewed Mohawk's white papers and topic wish list with a writer they knew well. Based on this review, the firm suggested a newly prioritized and logical structure for the series. The writer continued to work with Mohawk's production and marketing teams to develop the content, and became a "focus group of one." If she found something that was difficult to understand, this probably meant the text should be clarified. The team constantly asked, "How much information can we include to make the pieces useful but still accessible?" Schimmel says, "We didn't start designing until the content was nailed. Designing is a lot easier to do when

y to the printer—
s can take place

Before Uncoated Curves Adjusted

After Uncoated Curves Adjusted

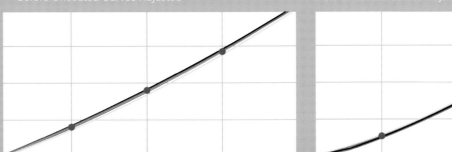

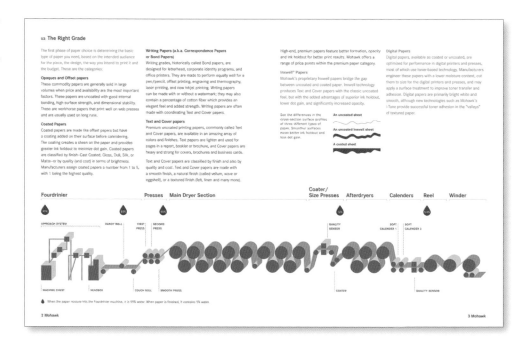

➜ Small illustrations were used for visual relief and to attract attention. Drawings and diagrams were consistently used to clarify content.

you know what you're saying. And having a piece where the design and the writing are integrated is the best way to get good information design."

Elegant Primers. The design team began to work with sample sections to present design schemes. Because they wanted the pieces to feel practical but look beautiful, each piece was designed in two colors, within an overall series palette. This simple palette also helped to guarantee the pieces would be easy to reproduce by various printers across the U.S.

The designers also wanted to use design elements to reinforce a sense of information architecture, so readers wouldn't be required to read any of the pieces from beginning to end. The design needed to function just as well for someone just flipping through.

To keep the pieces from feeling too technical, fields of color were used to "mix it up," providing contrast to pages with a lot of detail. Small illustrations add visual relief and attract attention. Consistent drawings and diagrams clarify content.

As the designers proceeded, they developed the system with a solid grid as well as detailed style sheets so it could be implemented by other design firms down the road.

Sellout Crowd. The response from the marketplace was enthusiastic. One of the first pieces was immediately reprinted to meet demand. Specific feedback indicated that designers loved how the pieces were straightforward, practical, and easy to use. And they appreciated the simple, elegant, geometric illustrations on the covers that branded the series, making it easy to find the brochures on a crowded bookshelf.

02: Continuous Tone: The Elusive Ideal
A photograph, painting or illustration that includes different shades or gradations of color is said to have continuous tone. The history of printing is a history of progress toward reproducing continuous tone in mass quantities. We are getting closer, but we're not there yet. Most printing processes still depend on the halftone's binary distinction between ink and no-ink portions of an image.
Finer Screens, Higher Resolutions
With halftones, the quality of the outcome—its ability to fool the eye into seeing continuous tone—depends on the size of the screen used to divide the image into dots.
Conventional halftone screens range in size from 60 lines of dots per inch (lpi) to 600. Like threads per inch in bedding, the higher the number, the finer the resolution or detail of the image. Smaller screens in the 60-85 lpi range have been commonly used in newspapers, where the results can be grainy. With screens of 133 or more lpi, the resulting dots are invisible to the naked eye. For high quality printing on premium paper, 175 lpi is considered the minimum standard line screen.
Stochastic Improvements
Over the years, more and more printers have given up film in favor of a direct-to-plate prepress process. Direct-to-plate allows the printers to offer stochastic screening, as well as conventional.
In the stochastic process, uniform-sized dots are placed randomly. Stochastic screens are measured in microns and refer to the size of the dot. Opposite to the system of conventional screen measurement, the lower the number of microns, the finer the resolution in the image.
A 10-micron stochastic screen produces an image equivalent to a 480-550 lpi conventional screen and a 20-micron stochastic screen is equivalent to a 380-400 lpi.
With stochastic screening, the number of dots determines the density of the color, in contrast to conventional screening where color density depends on the size of the dot.
Advantages of stochastic screening are:
• finer line screens (equivalent to 200 lpi and higher)
• easier and smoother tint builds
• ability to print more type out of screens without sawtooth edges
• no risk of moiré in angled areas of images
• no rosettes in flesh tones
• reduced dot gain
Disadvantages of stochastic screening include the printer's costs for special software and high-end plates as well as for the research and development required to fine tune the process for a particular press. Fine screens can also create a challenge on press; when you push ink to increase saturation in stochastic screened areas, you might see very little movement or gain, but the inks can become plugged and look mottled. Corrections may mean a return to prepress.
Today many printers use both stochastic and conventional screens, depending on the image. Either process can provide excellent results on uncoated papers.
STOCHASTIC: Arising from chance; random.
MOIRÉ: The appearance of patterns in an image caused by incorrect screen angles.
MOTTLED OR MOTTLING: Having a blotchy, cratered appearance similar to the lunar surface. Mottling is a risk for images that include big areas of solid color.
4 Mohawk
Stochastic (20 Micron/380 lpi)
Conventional Line Screen (175 lpi)
Line Screen Dot Pattern
60 DPI
120 DPI
175 DPI
200 DPI
250 DPI
300 DPI

In order for readers to feel that these pieces provide objective information, the designers have developed a color-coded system so that any text related to product advantages is highlighted in a second color. This helps readers identify the types of content they want to read.

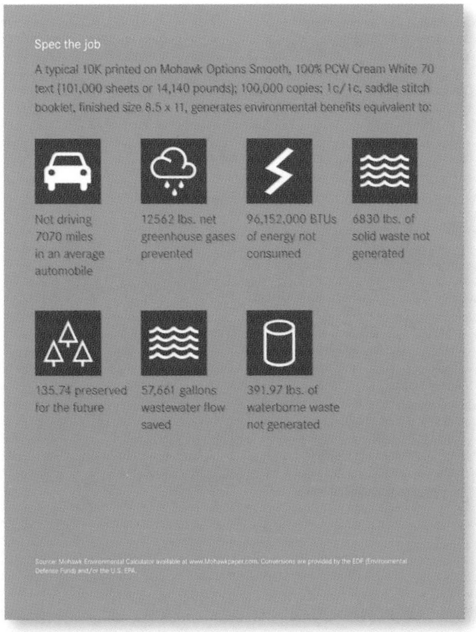
Spec the job
A typical 10K printed on Mohawk Options Smooth, 100% PCW Cream White 70 text (101,000 sheets or 14,140 pounds); 100,000 copies; 1c/1c, saddle stitch booklet, finished size 8.5 x 11, generates environmental benefits equivalent to:
Not driving 7070 miles in an average automobile
12562 lbs. net greenhouse gases prevented
96,152,000 BTUs of energy not consumed
6830 lbs. of solid waste not generated
135.74 preserved for the future
57,661 gallons wastewater flow saved
391.97 lbs. of waterborne waste not generated
Source: Mohawk Environmental Calculator available at www.Mohawkpaper.com. Conversions are provided by the EDF (Environmental Defense Fund) and/or the U.S. EPA.

The majority of paper promotions are extremely elaborate and color saturated. In order to put an emphasis on content, most of the Mohawk brochures were simply produced in two colors. This also helped to ensure the system would be easy to reproduce by printers across the U.S.

Graphic icons draw the eye to product benefit statements.

Information + Emotion = Innovation

Case Study
Sal. Oppenheim

Project
Magazine

Design Firm
Simon & Goetz Design

The German design firm of Simon & Goetz Design has the utmost respect for information design's core principles of simplicity and clarity, but that doesn't mean they won't play with your emotions too. "If one attempts to expand the levelheaded world of information by emotional dimensions, the communication often becomes more tangible and memorable for readers," explains Simon & Goetz art director Bernd Vollmöller.

Founded in 1789, one of Europe's leading independent private banks, Sal. Oppenheim, focuses on asset management and investment banking. The bank is a partner to prosperous private clients and corporate customers, helping them face the challenges of the financial market. The bank is known for its forward-thinking approach to business and communications.

In order to illustrate a complex topic, Simon & Goetz created an unusual but successful solution where the illustrations act as stories in their own right, carrying the core messaging of the article in a visually striking way.

Art and Culture Has a Place in Business.
Sal. Oppenheim's philosophy includes open-minded concern for new industrial and economic developments, sensitivity toward sociopolitical issues, and a strong commitment to art and culture. The goal: Ensure that an innovative approach translates loud and clear in their public relations and communications tools.

A Groundbreaking Magazine. Seeking to enter into a regular dialog with its clients, Sal. Oppenheim engaged Simon & Goetz to create a standout publication for sophisticated readers. Not satisfied with self-promotion, the bank intended to inspire their audiences with unexpected content, and to expand awareness by looking at familiar topics through a different lens. Now in its fifth year of publication, the magazine continues to engage clients, potential clients, and bank employees with thought-provoking content and cutting-edge information design.

"The magazine's design uses emotions to create reader enthusiasm for a topic or article," says Vollmöller. "The idea is to feature emotionally engaging images within the articles alongside the standard facts, figures, and diagrams to create a kind of collage." Each article features a design that is custom-tailored to the particular content. Design elements represent the core message of the article and provide information at the same time.

24,8%

Bis zu 10.000.000 Euro

4,7%

Bis zu 100.000.000 Euro

Provocative cover imagery helps distinguish the magazine from peer publications that take a more predictable approach.

Illustrated charts highlight issues of job loss and profitability when production jobs are moved out of Germany.

Why an Emotional Approach Works.

"Information today is a commercial product," says Vollmöller. "Nonetheless, the array of detailed yet redundant information from various sources prevents us from seeing the forest for the trees."

The magazine's distinctive look, combined with its wealth of information, has been a great success. "This approach to design has a very positive impact on a brand," he says. "The magazine has received multiple awards, but more importantly, it is truly appreciated by readers."

Great Relationships Yield Great Results.

The goal of any collaboration between designer and client is the development of a relationship and trust. Vollmöller says, "Gaining the client's trust that the content and goals of the magazine will continually be communicated in the most professional, brand-appropriate, and quality manner is the result of a continuous and collaborative development process."

Humans show a remarkable need to visualize, understand, and catalog the world around them. We have been mapping geographic landscapes for centuries. We create charts and diagrams to analyze data and draw conclusions from it. Well-executed information graphics create a sense of context and reveal relationships between sets of information, allowing for new and more nuanced conclusions.

INFORMATION GRAPHICS CASE STUDIES

6

→ Alejandro Tumas

→ The *New York Times*

→ Funnel Incorporated

→ White Rhino

→ Nigel Holmes

→ The *Wall Street Journal*

Inside Industrial Complexity

Case Study
Siderar

Project
Industrial Diagram

Designer
Alejandro Tumas

Argentinian company Siderar produces steel for a variety of purposes and industries. Their on-site blast furnace, inactive for nine years, was being revamped and reactivated for production. The process included the introduction of new and modified furnace parts. The company needed to create communication materials that showcased different engineering processes and specific technical issues to a nontechnical audience. Information graphics designer Alejandro Tumas was brought on to help Siderar tell its story in visual terms. Tumas' blast furnace infographic was part of the overall editorial coverage featured in a company report on the reinstallation and operation of the facility.

"Interact as much as you can with your client. Create the feeling of ownership in the client, and make sure they stay as excited as you are during the process." —Alejandro Tumas

Technical Concepts for General Audiences. "The challenge in creating the blast furnace infographic," explains Tumas, "was to turn something extremely complex into an understandable, attractive informative graphic, and to give a less sophisticated audience a better understanding of the technological innovations taking place within the company."

Another challenge in the project was working with the engineers. "It was clear that the engineers were the ones with the knowledge. We were just there to communicate it in a more appropriate manner. Specialists, whether they're doctors, physicians, or engineers, can be the most difficult clients. It is hard to make them understand that it is often necessary to omit many technical details. We weren't creating a thesis, but a graphic for everyday people."

The Road to Infographics. Tumas got his start working at Grupo Multimedios America in the design department on their newspaper, *El Cronista*. "The newspaper was my first encounter with the emerging discipline of infographics," says Tumas. "These types of graphics—very primitive, but with great impact—fascinated me."

He later became an infographics designer at the newspaper *Clarin*, where he eventually became department chief. "I created my

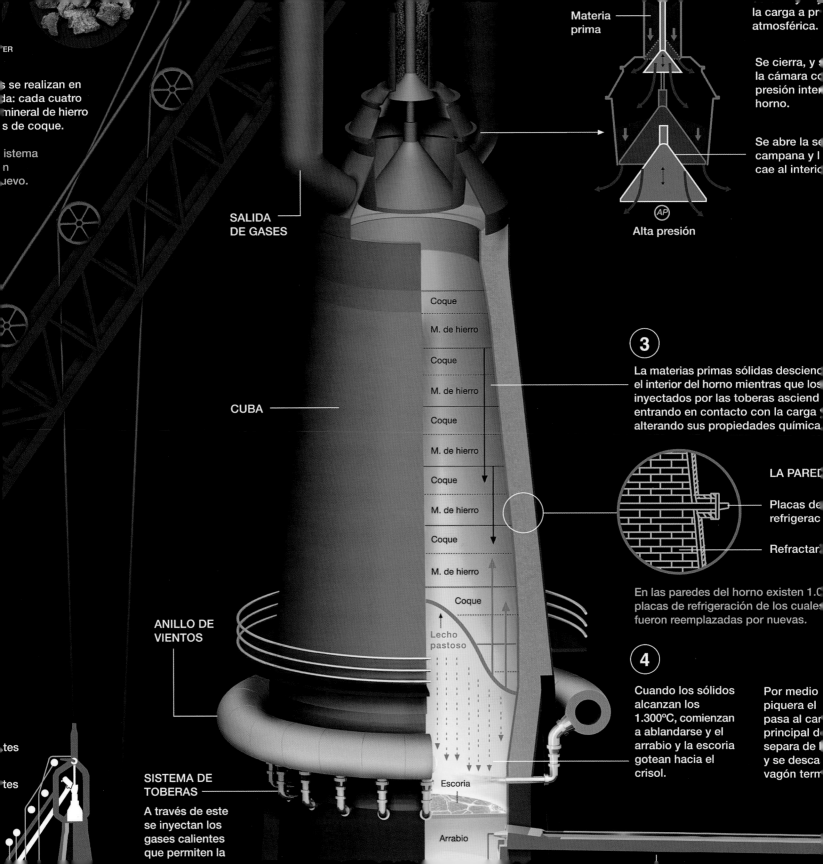

se realizan en
da: cada cuatro
mineral de hierro
s de coque.

istema
n
uevo.

Materia prima

la carga a pr
atmosférica.

Se cierra, y s
la cámara co
presión inter
horno.

Se abre la se
campana y l
cae al interic

(AP)

Alta presión

SALIDA DE GASES

CUBA

Coque
M. de hierro
Coque
M. de hierro
Coque
M. de hierro
Coque
M. de hierro
Coque
M. de hierro
Coque
Lecho pastoso

(3)

La materias primas sólidas descienc
el interior del horno mientras que los
inyectados por las toberas asciend
entrando en contacto con la carga y
alterando sus propiedades química.

LA PARED

Placas de
refrigerac

Refractar.

En las paredes del horno existen 1.0
placas de refrigeración de los cuales
fueron reemplazadas por nuevas.

(4)

Cuando los sólidos
alcanzan los
1.300°C, comienzan
a ablandarse y el
arrabio y la escoria
gotean hacia el
crisol.

Por medio
piquera el
pasa al car
principal d
separa de l
y se desca
vagón term

ANILLO DE VIENTOS

SISTEMA DE TOBERAS

A través de este
se inyectan los
gases calientes
que permiten la

Escoria

Arrabio

tes

tes

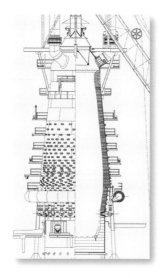

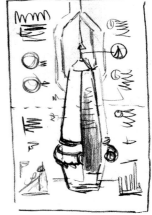

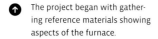

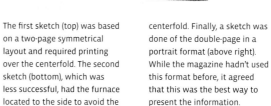

↑ The project began with gathering reference materials showing aspects of the furnace.

↑ This diagram of the production process was created as part of the research.

↑ The first sketch (top) was based on a two-page symmetrical layout and required printing over the centerfold. The second sketch (bottom), which was less successful, had the furnace located to the side to avoid the centerfold. Finally, a sketch was done of the double-page in a portrait format (above right). While the magazine hadn't used this format before, it agreed that this was the best way to present the information.

first infographics prototypes at *El Cronista*, but it was at *Clarin* that I was able to develop this discipline."

Tips from the Infographic Design Trenches. Tumas has learned a few things since he started doing infographics in the early '90s and has a few tips to share.

Learn Business Hierarchies. With complex projects, a designer often has more than one client contributing ideas. "With the blast furnace project there was a parade of engineers, each with their own agenda.

It was hard to please all of them," Tumas explains. "However, once we learned their hierarchies, it helped. If Juan was higher in the food chain, we would often defer to him in the process."

Keep the Client Close. "Interact as much as you can with your client," Tumas says. "Create the feeling of ownership in the client and make sure they stay as excited as you are during the process. The worst thing that can happen is a client becoming distanced from the project."

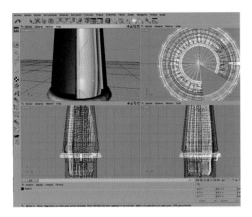

↑ A 3-D rendering was created using modeling software.

Negotiate Text Length. What do you do when a client delivers too much text to fit the graphic? Tumas has a negotiation process he sometimes uses. "We would plan for five lines of text and then give them a mock-up with only three lines. 'That's too short!' they would say and give us ten lines of text. We would show a final version with five lines of text and make the client believe we had compromised two more lines, even though we had planned five lines from the beginning," Tumas says.

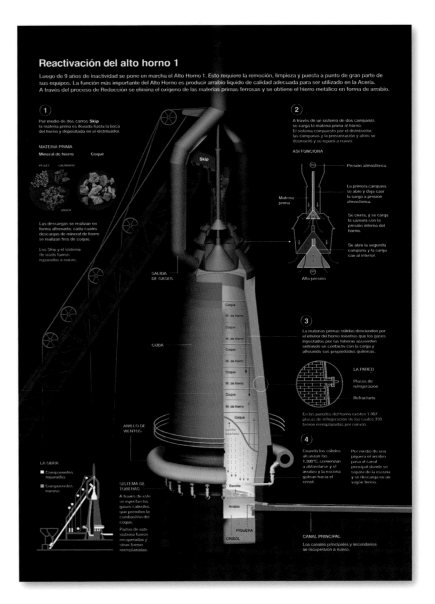

↑ Tumas' final infographic illustrates how the furnace works, and highlights new or modified furnace parts. Yellow highlighting and text on the graphic describe what was done to put the furnace back in operation, while white text and graphic elements explain how the furnace works.

Illuminating the News

Case Study
The *New York Times*

Project
Maps and Diagrams

Design Team
**The *New York Times*
Graphics Department**

Archie Tse grew up drawing airplanes and making sketches of mechanical devices, so it made sense that he enrolled as a mechanical engineering major when he went to college. Except, he confesses, he failed his engineering classes, because by that time he'd found another passion—working at the student newspaper. The paper had been looking for a graphic artist, and Tse took the bait.

Years later, Tse may have the perfect job to marry his two passions. He is a highly respected graphics editor at the *New York Times*. "As an engineering student I had to produce drawings for what I wanted to build. And in lab classes, I enjoyed finding ways to present experimental data."

> **"To really understand a data set, you need to process it yourself. Seventy-five percent of our time is spent reporting, gathering, and distilling information."**
>
> —Archie Tse

A Mindset for the Job. Tse says that many of the graphics editors at the *Times* have scientific or mathematical backgrounds. "To really understand a data set, you need to process it yourself. Seventy-five percent of our time is spent reporting, gathering, and distilling information," Tse explains. "But we also need people who are experts in visualizing the information."

Tse recalls when one of the *Times'* best investigative correspondents needed to file a sweeping overview of the war in Afghanistan. When it came time to think about an appropriate visual, it was clear photography wasn't going to work. The visual had to communicate an overarching and historical perspective, so an information graphic was more appropriate. The graphic was designed to complement the reporting and provide the kind of information a written story couldn't convey.

From the Field. "In order to create really good graphics, you have to have really good information. You have to immerse yourself in the subject and do your own reporting. It was hard to get good information second-hand, so the *Times* sent me to Iraq in 2003," Tse recalls. He also traveled to Lebanon in 2006 to cover the war there. Tse filed video

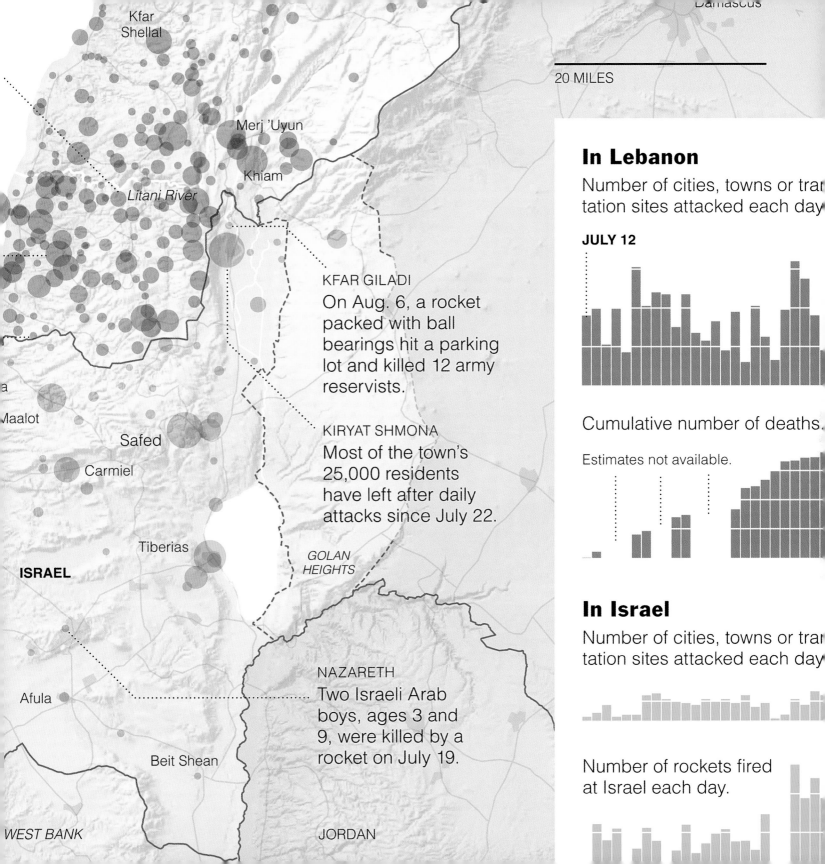

Kfar
Shellal

Merj 'Uyun

Khiam

Litani River

Maalot

Safed

Carmiel

Tiberias

ISRAEL

*GOLAN
HEIGHTS*

Afula

NAZARETH
Two Israeli Arab
boys, ages 3 and
9, were killed by a
rocket on July 19.

Beit Shean

WEST BANK

JORDAN

Damascus

20 MILES

KFAR GILADI
On Aug. 6, a rocket
packed with ball
bearings hit a parking
lot and killed 12 army
reservists.

KIRYAT SHMONA
Most of the town's
25,000 residents
have left after daily
attacks since July 22.

In Lebanon
Number of cities, towns or tran
tation sites attacked each day

JULY 12

Cumulative number of deaths.

Estimates not available.

In Israel
Number of cities, towns or tran
tation sites attacked each day

Number of rockets fired
at Israel each day.

reports and worked with colleagues in Jerusalem and New York to produce graphics for the website. "Interactive graphics require a different visual tool set than print graphics," he says. He also notes that the opportunity to learn new things is what he likes best about the job.

All for One. Graphics editors at the *Times* all have different strengths, be it reporting, working with databases, 3-D rendering, or Flash. "Our skill sets complement each other, so we will often bring two or three people together on a project." As a department, he says, they are constantly searching for ways that graphics can support stories. "We want to help people understand what is going on. We know it's a balancing act. We need to provide enough detail to illuminate the content, but showing too much complexity may alienate some readers," Tse explains.

Tse and his team feel a tremendous responsibility to get it right. "You err on the side of showing less. You have to let the data speak for itself." Tse feels best about the instances when they have worked hard on graphics to help people understand the nuances of data sets. He notes some of the map graphics they published to help readers understand aspects of the U.S. presidential elections, where things aren't always as black and white, or in this case, red or blue, as they might seem.

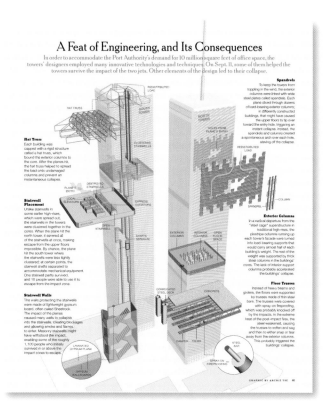

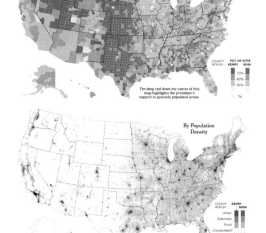

● This detailed rendering shows important aspects in the engineering of the World Trade Center buildings. The rendering's "inside view" is clarified with callouts.

→ "The 2000 presidential election in the U.S. was the first time we could take advantage of new computational software that would let us analyze voting by county, and still make our deadline. The maps we ran become rather iconic in the public discourse because they allowed people to understand the elections in a more nuanced, or shaded, way."

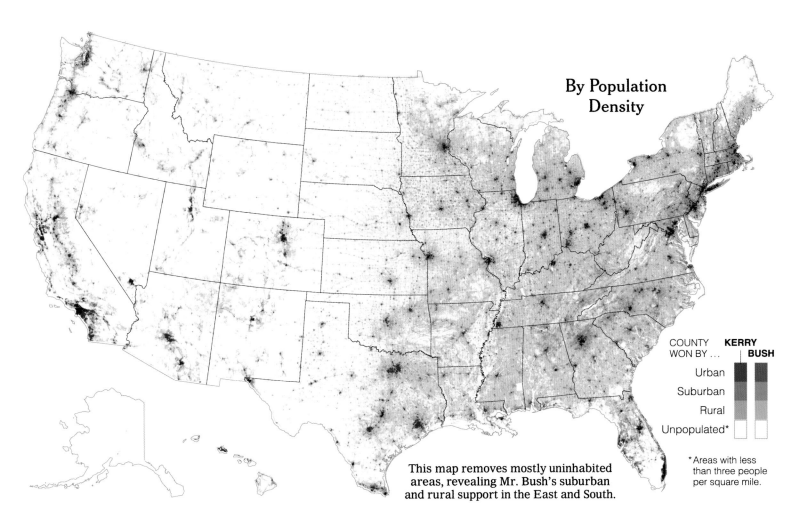

By Population
Density

COUNTY
WON BY ...   KERRY
              BUSH

Urban
Suburban
Rural
Unpopulated*

*Areas with less
than three people
per square mile.

This map removes mostly uninhabited
areas, revealing Mr. Bush's suburban
and rural support in the East and South.

"Other publications had published maps that recorded the wins by state with solid colors, indicating only wins and losses. By using more subtle shading, people could visualize the dynamics, factoring for the ways population density affected the results. In the end, it showed the election had been won by a whisper in terms of total votes. It was all about the narrow margin," says Tse.

No Need to Dumb It Down

Case Study
Various

Project
Various

Design Firm
Funnel Incorporated

One thing that information graphics designers Lori and Lin Wilson, of Funnel Incorporated, love is that their practice gives them leave to ask dumb questions. "I'll be in front of engineers who are throwing lingo around the room and I feel like I have permission to say, 'I don't know what that means,' over and over again," explains Lin.

Not knowing what something means, but finding out and then depicting it in clear, concise, visual terms is what Funnel does best. Since 2002, Funnel has been designing infographics, icons, maps, and instructions, with the ultimate goal of advocating for the end user.

"I feel like I have permission to say, 'I don't know what that means,' over and over again."—Lin Wilson

Playing Dumb. "Our deliverable is understanding," says Lin. "Clients usually call us because there's something their customers can't understand. We chase the most confusing parts of the client's story first."

"We work hard to make our clients understand that what we're doing is clarifying and not dumbing down," adds Lori. "We say we're dumb, but really, we're generalists and we use that to our advantage so that we can learn."

Most of the folks at Funnel come from branding, marketing, public relations, and advertising backgrounds. "Our work is practical. All we do is information design. I'm perfecting my background of 'whittling,' so to speak. I used to whittle words, now I whittle information. But it's the same process," says Lori.

From Brain to Whiteboard. Gathering essential information is a process that can take different forms. "There are the 'Give us everything you've got' conference calls," explains Lin. "Sometimes clients give us existing brochures or really awful PowerPoint presentations. Often, there are nuggets buried in bad design."

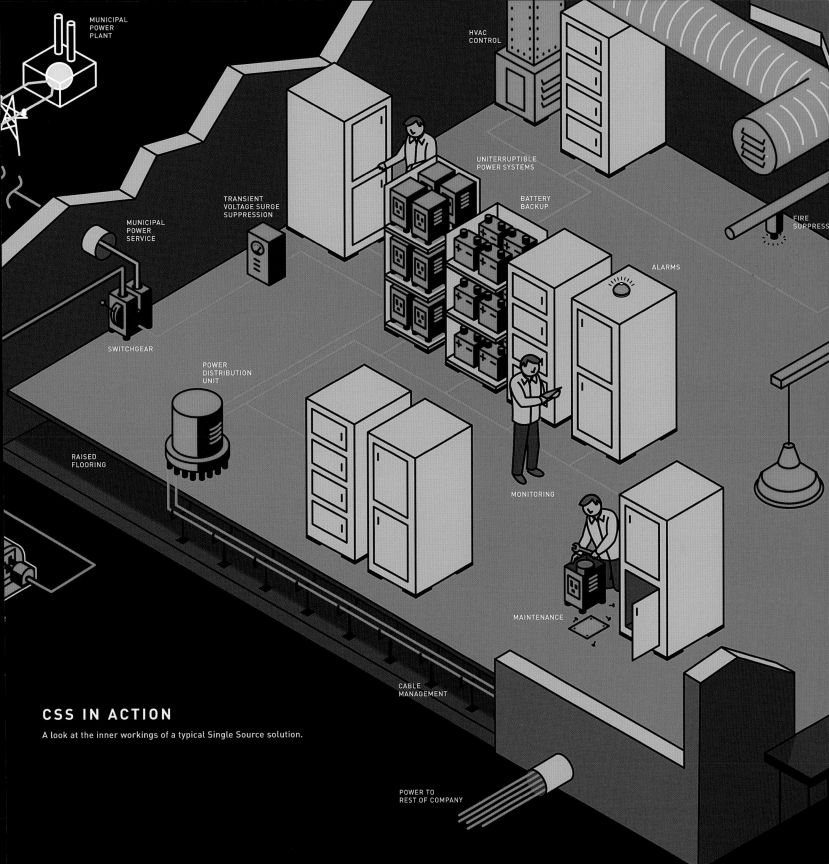

MUNICIPAL
POWER
PLANT

HVAC
CONTROL

MUNICIPAL
POWER
SERVICE

TRANSIENT
VOLTAGE SURGE
SUPPRESSION

UNITERRUPTIBLE
POWER SYSTEMS

BATTERY
BACKUP

FIRE
SUPPRESS

ALARMS

SWITCHGEAR

POWER
DISTRIBUTION
UNIT

RAISED
FLOORING

MONITORING

MAINTENANCE

CABLE
MANAGEMENT

CSS IN ACTION

A look at the inner workings of a typical Single Source solution.

POWER TO
REST OF COMPANY

Environmental advocacy client Clean Wisconsin needed to educate Wisconsin's editors about the issues surrounding the Great Lakes water supply. The graphic was prominently featured in a comprehensive press kit, and was also included as part of the organization's newsletter and on their website.

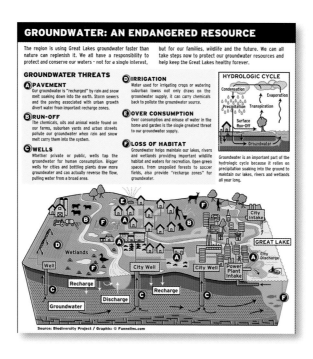

"Whiteboard sessions get very interesting because they can include a lot of people on the client side who may be in disagreement," says Lori. "What's nice about the whiteboard and the sketches we do is that we're providing a dartboard. Clients have something they can react to. It's messy and it's ugly, and it's really fun because eventually everybody has to agree."

During these sessions, Funnel blurs the territorial line between client and creative. "The client gets handed the pen too. The goal of everybody in the room is to get the story right. A whiteboard drawing session can almost be its own deliverable," says Lin.

Funnel Incorporated created this infographic for client Biodiversity Project's press kit. The graphic helped the organization communicate the complex issue of Great Lakes polluted groundwater to editors. Many publications no longer have photographers or illustrators on staff, so infographics such as these help increase the odds of media placement and lend credibility to a story.

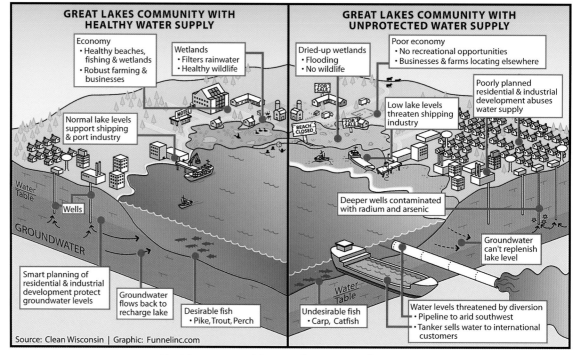

Healthy communities need water supply protection.

> **"Our deliverable is understanding. Clients usually call us because there's something their customers can't understand. We chase the most confusing parts of the client's story first."** —Lin Wilson

Putting Infographics on the Map. How did infographics pick up steam in the world of designed communication? "As PowerPoint became much more widespread, we saw so many failed attempts at describing complex material," says Lin. "Concurrently, Edward Tufte started presenting his information design seminars, helping to put information design in the budget pie chart of corporate America."

Funnel often creates infographics for their clients to pitch to newspapers and magazines, and has a great success rate getting the attention of editors. "You have a time-pressed editor just as you have time-pressed readers. Editors are buried in press kits," explains Lori. "If you're trying to place a story with an editor, information graphics are a great way to cut through the clutter and ensure that he or she understands the potential story."

Editors don't have enough photographers or illustrators on staff anymore, so to provide a powerful graphic that they can just plug in can be incredibly helpful—and memorable. "Editors say, 'Oh yeah, we remember you. You sent that really cool infographic!' which can ultimately result in more story placements," says Lori.

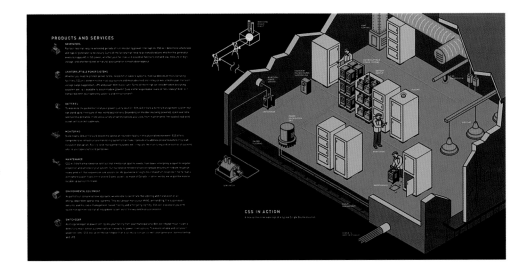

↑ Icons are embedded into the CSS Power diagram to represent each component of the system. These icons work as an ensemble. Individually, the icons provide the client with a set of useful hieroglyphics symbolizing each product or service.

↑ Funnel Incorporated worked closely with the client's design agency, Planet Propaganda, to craft an image telling the entire story of CSS Power's backup power solutions.

A Passion for Mapping

Case Study
History Shots

Project
**Large-scale
Infographic Prints**

Design Firm
White Rhino

There are some who might find Bill Yonker and Larry Gormley a bit fanatical. Partners in History Shots, the two create complex, elegant information graphics based on history, politics, and sports. As the son of a map collector, Gormley admits he grew up admiring maps of all kinds. He says he's the one who loves looking into "deep history." In the meantime, he describes Yonker as the one who asks the "big questions," a current events, sports, and outdoors guy. As a way to capitalize on these passions, they designed a business that would publish their obsessions as beautiful prints. They each work on two to three ideas for projects at any given time, and spend at least three to four months researching each topic.

"We feel there's always an 'aha moment' as we sift through the data, where we find the story to be told." —Larry Gormley

Searching for the Aha Moment. After all the collecting, the two partners say the hardest task is "peeling away the density of data." As they work, they write the words "What is the story?" in large letters at the top of their worksheets as a constant reminder to find the very essence of the narrative. "We feel there's always an 'aha moment' as we sift through the data, where we find the story to be told," says Gormley. After all the winnowing, it's likely that only 25 percent of the total data will be used for any given subject. History Shots uses its website as a way to add value, publishing a lot of the information that would have been too overwhelming to incorporate into any one print.

An Iterative Process. Since the first print in 2004, History Shots has been collaborating with the graphic design firm White Rhino. The team has worked together long enough that roles are not hard and fast. Gormley and Yonker bring drafts and sketches. They rely on White Rhino to help them "kick the tires" and make suggestions for the best ways to depict and organize various aspects of the data/storytelling. As a team, they will often go through a dozen graphic scenarios before they feel they've found the right way to organize the data. It's often the relationship between disparate types of data that creates the biggest revelations.

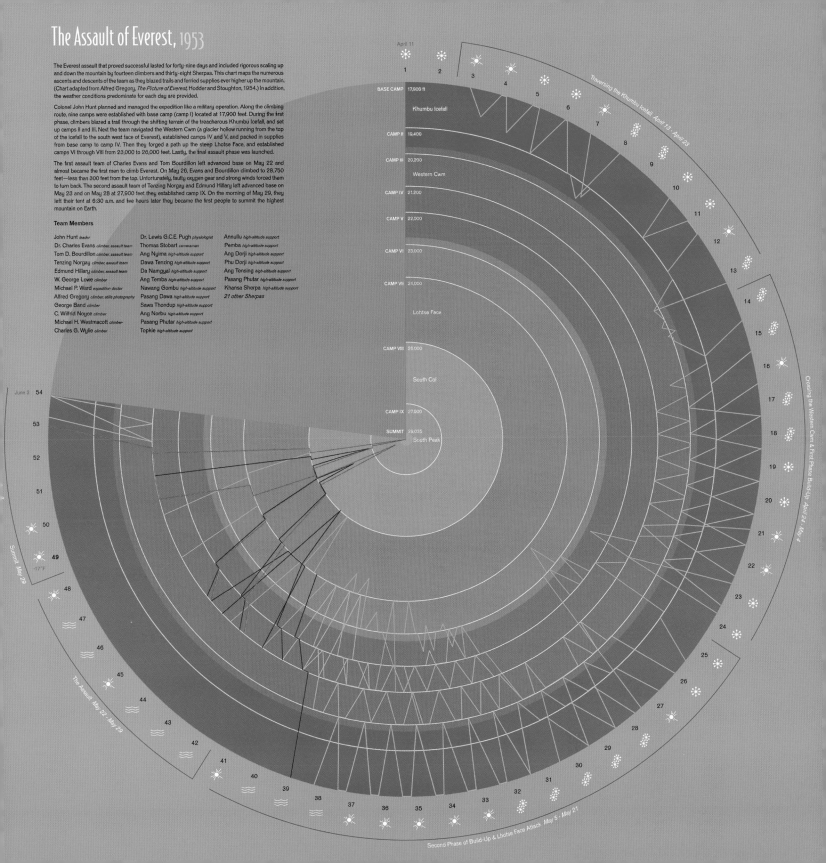

The Assault of Everest, 1953

The Everest assault that proved successful lasted for forty-nine days and included rigorous scaling up and down the mountain by fourteen climbers and thirty-eight Sherpas. This chart maps the numerous ascents and descents of the team as they blazed trails and ferried supplies ever higher up the mountain. (Chart adapted from Alfred Gregory, *The Picture of Everest*, Hodder and Stoughton, 1954.) In addition, the weather conditions predominate for each day are provided.

Colonel John Hunt planned and managed the expedition like a military operation. Along the climbing route, nine camps were established with base camp (camp I) located at 17,900 feet. During the first phase, climbers blazed a trail through the shifting terrain of the treacherous Khumbu Icefall, and set up camps II and III. Next the team navigated the Western Cwm (a glacier hollow running from the top of the icefall to the south west face of Everest), established camps IV and V, and packed in supplies from base camp to camp IV. Then they forged a path up the steep Lhotse Face, and established camps VI through VIII from 23,000 to 26,000 feet. Lastly, the final assault phase was launched.

The first assault team of Charles Evans and Tom Bourdillon left advanced base on May 22 and almost became the first men to climb Everest. On May 26, Evans and Bourdillon climbed to 28,750 feet—less than 300 feet from the top. Unfortunately, faulty oxygen gear and strong winds forced them to turn back. The second assault team of Tenzing Norgay and Edmund Hillary left advanced base on May 23 and on May 28 at 27,900 feet they established camp IX. On the morning of May 29, they left their tent at 6:30 a.m. and five hours later they became the first people to summit the highest mountain on Earth.

Team Members

John Hunt *leader*	Dr. Lewis G.C.E. Pugh *physiologist*	Annullu *high-altitude support*
Dr. Charles Evans *climber, assault team*	Thomas Stobart *cameraman*	Pemba *high-altitude support*
Tom D. Bourdillon *climber, assault team*	Ang Nyima *high-altitude support*	Phu Dorji *high-altitude support*
Tenzing Norgay *climber, assault team*	Dawa Tenzing *high-altitude support*	Ang Tensing *high-altitude support*
Edmund Hillary *climber, assault team*	Da Namgyal *high-altitude support*	Pasang Phutar *high-altitude support*
W. George Lowe *climber*	Ang Temba *high-altitude support*	Khansa Sherpa *high-altitude support*
Michael P. Ward *expedition doctor*	Nawang Gombu *high-altitude support*	*21 other Sherpas*
Alfred Gregory *climber, stills photography*	Pasang Dawa *high-altitude support*	
George Band *climber*	Sawa Thondup *high-altitude support*	
C. Wilfrid Noyce *climber*	Ang Norbu *high-altitude support*	
Michael H. Westmacott *climber*	Pasang Phutar *high-altitude support*	
Charles G. Wylie *climber*	Topkie *high-altitude support*	

BASE CAMP 17,900 ft
Khumbu Icefall
CAMP II 19,400
CAMP III 20,200
Western Cwm
CAMP IV 21,200
CAMP V 22,000
CAMP VI 23,000
CAMP VII 24,000
Lohtse Face
CAMP VIII 26,000
South Col
CAMP IX 27,900
SUMMIT 29,035
South Peak

April 11

Traversing the Khumbu Icefall, April 13 - April 23

Crossing the Western Cwm & First Phase Build-Up, April 24 - May 4

Second Phase of Build-Up & Lhotse Face Attack, May 5 - May 21

The Assault, May 22 - May 29

Summit, May 29, -17°F

June 3

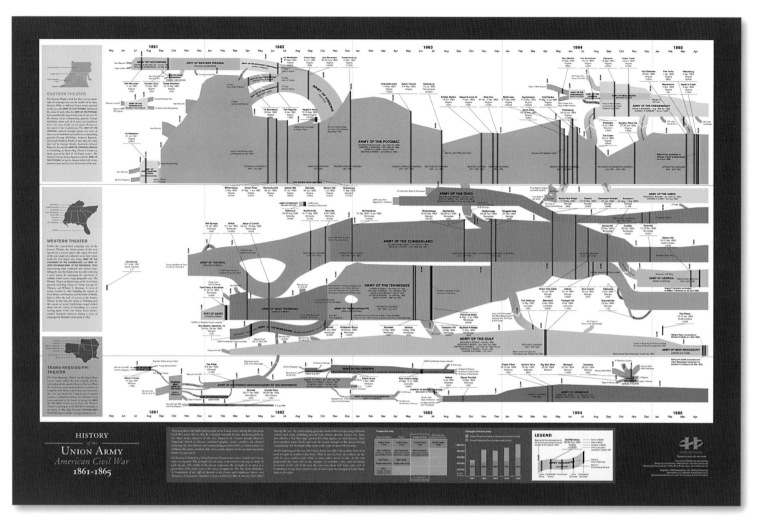

This poster maps the history of the Union Army during the American Civil War. Divided vertically by date, and horizontally by the three major theaters of the war, many variables are charted, including the size, history, and commanding generals of the thirty-one Union armies. In addition, the name, location, date, and casualty figures are provided for the ninety-five most important battles.

This detail from the map above shows the level of typographic complexity included in each of the posters.

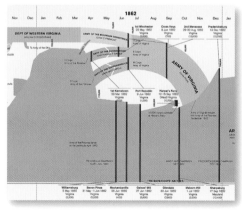

The goal is to tell the story with an economy of means, and with as little text as possible. "We try to get it to a place where there's no need for explanation," says Kimberly Cloutier, the designer at White Rhino. They informally test the graphics to make sure they "read."

The Devil's in the Details. White Rhino believes that using a more subdued color palette can sometimes make the information easier to absorb. They've found that too much color can be distracting with such density. Without relying on bright colors for information hierarchy at such a small scale, the attention to typography becomes even more critical. And the team is very diligent about specifying inks, papers, and even the kind of press that must be used because reproducing the fine detail is so critical.

Each of the prints is targeted to a specific audience. For instance, it might be a person deeply interested in the Civil War, or someone fascinated by the many attempts made to scale the top of Everest. On the other hand, the History Shots partners have found that there are many types of people attracted to their work. "There are so many people fascinated by mapping," says Gormley.

The team says the collaboration between White Rhino and History Shots has been successful because it is based on a mutual obsession with the projects. They add, "We just never run out of steam."

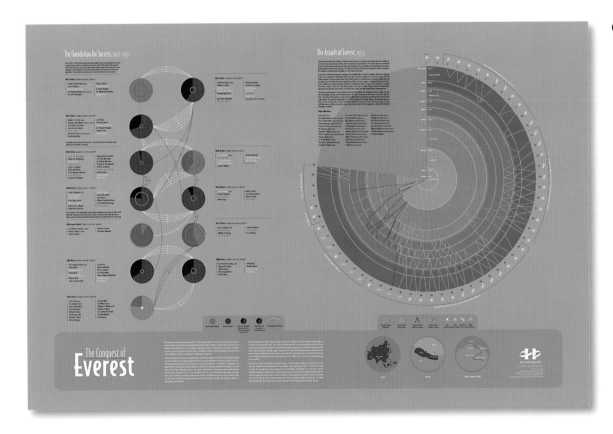

This print maps the conquest of Mount Everest from 1921 to 1953. The information on the left shows the year, sponsor, duration, dates, height reached, and members of each of the major expeditions. The graphic also tracks the history of climbers who went on more than one expedition. On the right is a detailed graph of the numerous ascents and descents of the 1953 team as they blazed trails and ferried supplies up the mountain. Weather conditions for each day are also provided.

A Crisis of Global Proportions

Case Study
Blue Planet Foundation

Project
Book Infographics

Designer
Nigel Holmes

Global water shortages may be the biggest crisis facing the world today. The lack of clean drinking water affects one in six people globally, and water-related illnesses are the leading cause of human sickness and death.

Blue Planet Run, a nonstop, around-the-world relay race, was organized by the Blue Planet Foundation to raise awareness about the crisis, and to generate funding. With twenty runners covering 15,200 miles (24,462.0 km) in ninety-five days, the logistics were masterminded by a firm that has organized six Olympic Torch Relays. The foundation teamed with Rick Smolan to create a large-format book of photography to document and broaden the run's reach.

"I always have to figure out which bits are better said in pictures and which are better said in words. And then I have to think about how to do both concisely."

—Nigel Holmes

The Human Face. Photographer Rick Smolan has a history of creating global photography projects that put a human face on geopolitical issues. These projects have collectively generated billions of media impressions worldwide, and four of his books have been *New York Times* bestsellers.

In planning the Blue Planet Run book, Smolan knew information graphics could help explain the complex issues in a way that readers would absorb. Smolan approached Nigel Holmes to create graphic spreads to introduce each of the book's eight chapters. In a sense, these spreads served as visual summaries.

Explanation Graphics. As a young illustration intern at the *London Sunday Times,*

Holmes was famously told by one of his bosses that he had a "knack for explaining things to people." And, in fact, he has had a long history of explaining things. After a very long stint as the graphics director at *TIME* magazine, he created his own firm, Explanation Graphics, and the name tidily states exactly what he's done for just about every major news publication in the world. Many of his peers credit him with transforming the way publications and corporations have come to use graphics to convey important information.

Holmes was drawn to working on the Blue Planet Run project. He threw himself into research, reading everything he could about

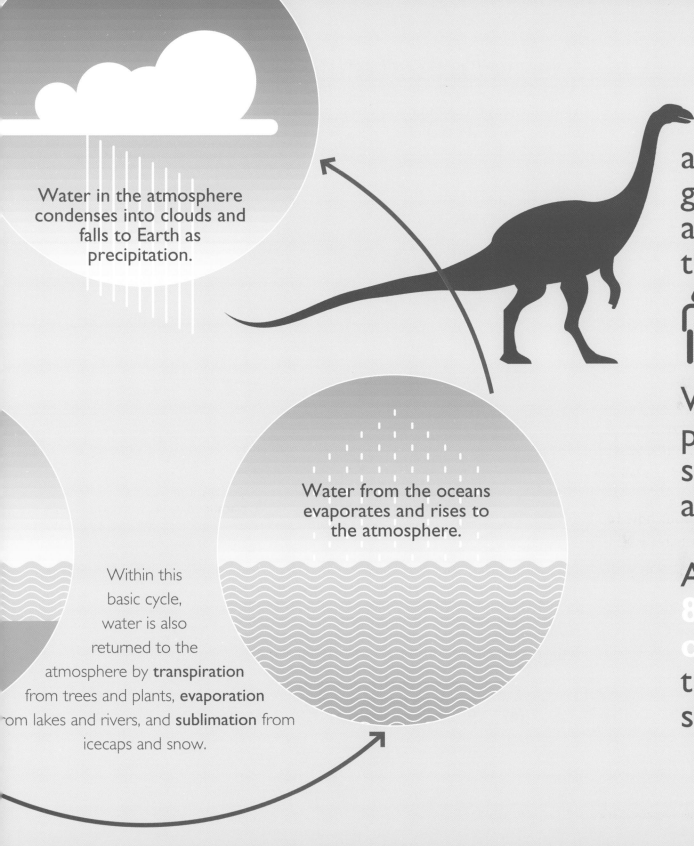

Water in the atmosphere condenses into clouds and falls to Earth as precipitation.

Water from the oceans evaporates and rises to the atmosphere.

Within this basic cycle, water is also returned to the atmosphere by **transpiration** from trees and plants, **evaporation** from lakes and rivers, and **sublimation** from icecaps and snow.

So if the amount o goes arou around, w the proble

US

We are w polluting t supply of v alarming r

And there 85 millio of us eac trying to g share of it

"The designer, Michael Rylander, and I decided very early in the process that a fairly minimal and monochromatic approach to the illustrations would work best in a richly photographic book. Blue was the obvious choice." —Nigel Holmes

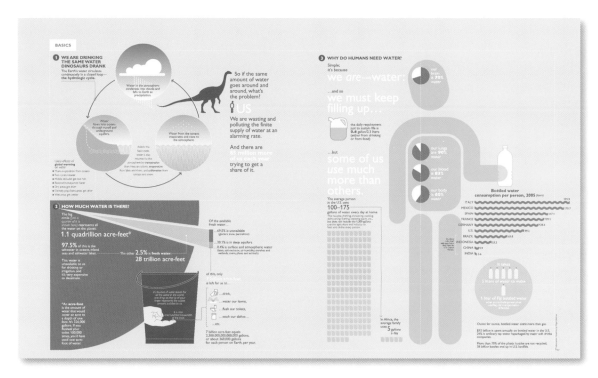

Holmes created a framing device to give the spreads a graphic consistency as they were scattered throughout the large-format book.

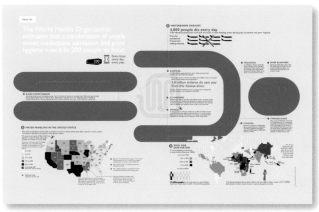

Holmes says, "I like the physical act of drawing and I always come back to it."

the issue. He says that in order to create a good piece of work he will often start with four times more information than he'll ultimately use. The editing is critical.

The Power of the Pictorial. Once Holmes was immersed in the data, he began to sketch. "I'm interested in pictures of information. You've got to get people interested, and people are intrigued by pictures," he says. But writing has also become more and more important in his work. He says, "I've been making my work a lot simpler lately. It allows me to spend more time thinking and less time drawing. I'm trying to get better at integrating the words so you have to read both things. I always have to figure out which bits are better said in pictures and which are better said in words. And then I have to think about how to do both concisely."

Graphic Narratives. Holmes talks about the passion he had for comics as a kid. His approach to the Blue Planet Run project clearly draws on that love for graphic narrative, as well as all the expertise Holmes has gained from years of wrestling with complex content. It's all been in the service of getting something concise but fantastically informative.

He explains, "I've gotten to the stage now where I don't want to waste time. I want to make everything count. I want to do projects that can make a difference."

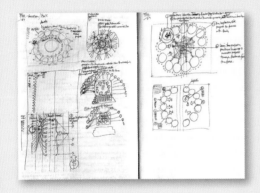

↑ "In a way, my drawings are becoming like pieces of type. Some are drawn for particular assignments. Some are taken from my files. I've been building a vocabulary I can use. They're a shorthand I can use to replace words." says Holmes.

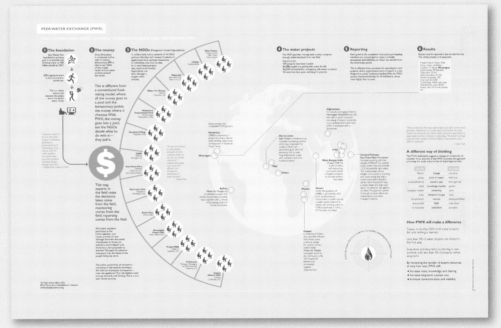

↑ Holmes knew the layout of each spread would need to be unique as he grouped the relevant pieces of information.

Attention to Detail

Case Study
The *Wall Street Journal*

Project
News Infographics

Design Team
**The *Wall Street Journal*
Information Graphics Department**

Dona Wong studied advanced mathematics and economics in college, but her dad was an artist, and there must have been some of that in her DNA because she ended up with a degree in graphic design. She explains it was the attention to detail that she loved about both worlds.

While she was in design school at Yale, the head of the department introduced her to Edward Tufte. Originally a professor of public policy, by that time he was refining his unique approach to information design from within Yale's design program. Wong was drawn to a pursuit that combined content, design, and a need for analytical skills.

For a year after graduating, Wong worked for a large accounting firm, helping them design presentations for their international clients. She says 99 percent of her job was crunching the numbers.

"At the end of the day, a good information designer needs to know their subject, and have a passion for it." —Dona Wong

The Fast Pace of a Newspaper. After her start in high finance, Wong's design DNA came into play again when she went to work at the *New York Times* as a graphics editor for the business section.

Know It in Your Sleep. Now at the *Wall Street Journal*, Wong thinks of herself primarily as a reporter. She says things have changed since she first began working in the field. "At the beginning, information design was still considered rather cosmetic. But now, graphics editors know their content deeply. They are constantly poring over data." At the *Journal*, the graphics editors are assigned to "beats," so they can really develop an expertise. "You can't know everything about everything, but if you're in commodities, you know it in your sleep," Wong notes.

The process of developing information graphics at the *Journal* is quite collaborative. Reporters, editors, and graphics editors come together to figure out the best way to tell a story. Often graphics editors will develop their own graphic stories. "You discover something you think the reader would want to know. You write a proposal. You may include a few bullet points or a sketch, and you pitch it to the editors just like any other reporter. At the end of the day, a good information designer needs to know their subject, and have a passion for it," Wong explains.

Two Sides of the Same Brain. "You have to do your own research," she says. "It's when I pore over the data that I start to picture the presentation and know whether it will work

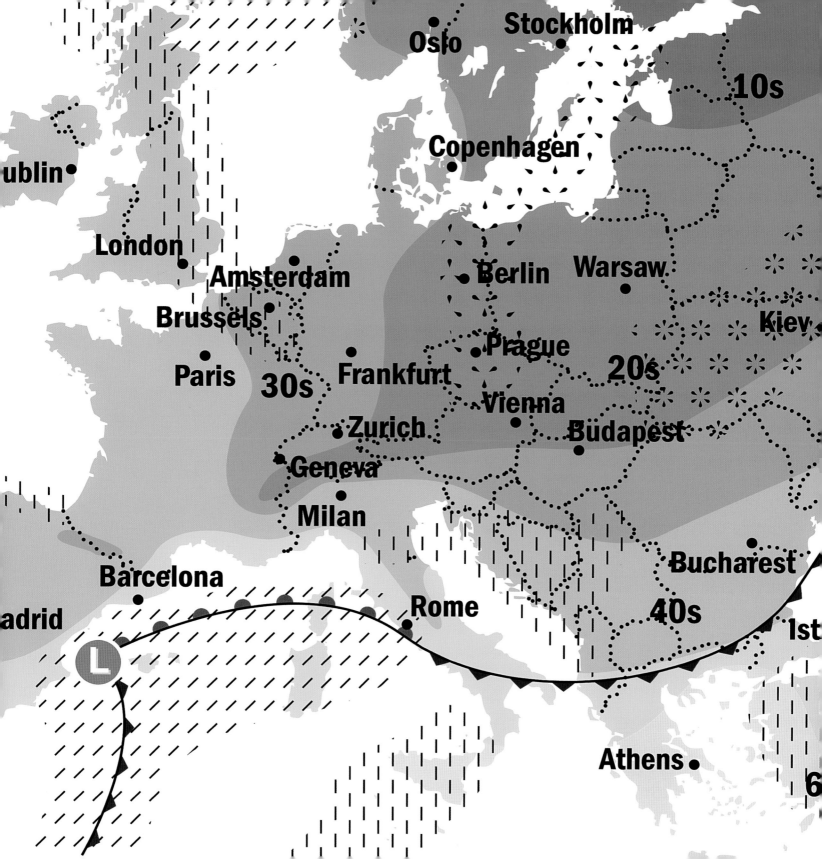

or not. And sometimes the data may not tell the story. A good information designer also has to know when to walk away."

The extremely complex world of finance makes it particularly difficult to find the right people for the job. The *Journal* often hires people with a background in finance, math, economics, or journalism, and trains them in the art of information design.

Wong says, "It really takes both sides of your brain. On one hand you have to think analytically, but you also have to find an inviting way to bring your viewer into the subject matter."

Wong says she still loves the fast pace of working on a daily newspaper. "Stories may arrive as late as an hour before the deadline, so you learn to be quick on your feet. And even when you have the story and the data, the space that's available is constantly changing." She says this is where good graphics editing really comes to play. "At the *Journal*, if the information graphic needs to get larger, we add content. We don't just increase the size to fill the space. At a design firm, you're given the content," Wong says. "Here you have to go find it."

→ Wong says, "On one hand you have to think analytically, but you also have to find an inviting way to bring your viewer into the subject matter."

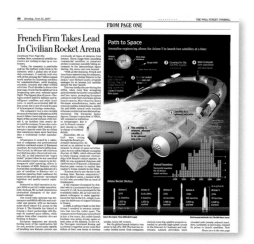

↑ Reporters, editors, and graphics editors come together to figure out the best way to tell a story. Often, graphics editors will develop their own graphic stories.

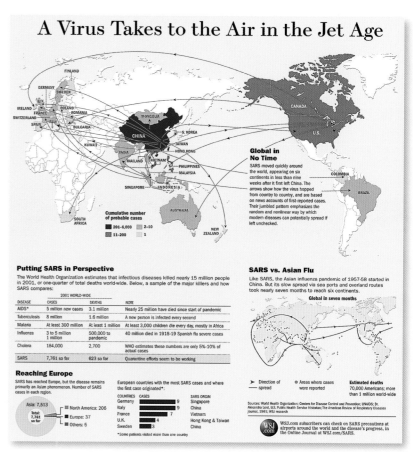

Screen-based experiences give users multiple ways of exploring content. Sometimes it's necessary to curate the experience and give people structured pathways. Other times the design needs to accommodate multiple entry points. Information design for interactive systems is a complex task and the field is in a constant and rapid state of evolution. Without a doubt, multilayered interactive systems demand well-conceived information design.

INTERACTIVE CASE STUDIES

7

→ **Hello Design**

→ **Sullivan**

→ **Second Story Interactive Studios/ Ralph Appelbaum Associates**

→ **VSA Partners**

→ **Kahn + Associates**

→ **frog design**

Virtual City Adventures

Case Study
LA Conservancy

Project
Website

Design Firm
Hello Design

Hello Design is dedicated to the creation of "intelligent, living systems." A good example is the site they developed for Curating the City, a program developed by the Los Angeles Conservancy. As the largest membership-based local historic preservation organization in the country, the Conservancy is dedicated to the architectural heritage of Los Angeles—a city often chastised for its tendency to blithely tear down historic buildings to "make way for the new."

Partially funded with a grant from the Getty Foundation, the website was designed as a companion to a month-long series of educational events exploring historic sites built along Wilshire Boulevard, the 16-mile (25.74-km) backbone that extends from downtown Los Angeles to the beach.

"Buried treasure has no value. There's no success if you create great content and no one can find it." —David Lai

Content Is King. Hello Design begins every project by defining what the team is trying to accomplish and identifying the challenges to be overcome. Originally conceived by the client as a short-lived virtual companion for the architectural tours, Hello Design worked with historians at the Conservancy to understand the value of the content and to explore what visitors would find most interesting. By asking questions, they hoped to make the website even more useful. The site needed to appeal to architectural enthusiasts, but also work for the general public, including teachers and their high school students. "It's important to embrace the content, and ask questions about things the client might take for granted," says Hello Design cofounder David Lai.

Lai and his cofounder, Hiro Niwa, came from large Web companies where the task and job description of information architecture was frequently its own "silo." They try to avoid this approach. "We believe it's crucial for designers to intimately understand information architecture. Otherwise, they rely on somebody else to think things through and lose huge opportunities to think innovatively about structure and navigation," says Lai.

Buried Treasure Has No Value. Hello Design works with the philosophy that effective information graphics help users find information as quickly as possible, even if

CURATING THE CITY:
WILSHIRE BLVD.

EXPLORE THE BLVD.

CURATING THE CITY   EVENTS
THE TOUR   FOR KIDS
MEMORY BOOK   FOR TEACHERS

LOS ANGELES
CONSERVANCY

Photos: Jim McHugh

EXPLORE THE BLVD

Take an interactive journey down one of L.A.'s most fascinating streets. From Victorian mansions to modern skyscrapers, Wilshire Boulevard has seen it all. You can, too, by creating your own customized tours of Wilshire's past and present.

BEGIN EXPLORING

MEMORY BOOK

What does Wilshire mean to you? Read personal stories of life along the boulevard, and submit your own.

➔ VIEW MEMORY BOOK

CURATING THE CITY

Learn about the Los Angeles Conservancy's exciting new educational program, which treats the city as a living museum by showcasing one aspect of our historic built environment.

➔ OVERVIEW

"We believe it's crucial for designers to intimately understand information architecture. Otherwise they rely on somebody else to think things through and lose huge opportunities to think innovatively about structure and navigation." —David Lai

Visitors can customize and print maps they can take along with them to use during an actual walking tour.

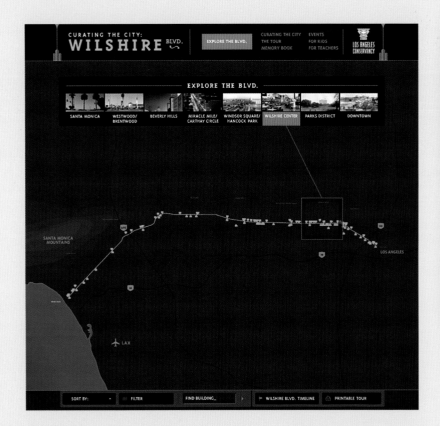

The site's centerpiece is "Explore the Boulevard," a richly detailed virtual tour. The interactive mapping allows users to explore neighborhoods in a general way, or drill down into details about specific buildings.

these users don't know exactly what they're looking for. "Search implies you know what you're looking for, but browsing lets you explore what's there. Good design needs to accommodate both. You won't succeed if you've created great content but no one can find it," Lai notes.

Hello Design talks to its clients about "information rationing"—using bite-sized pieces of information on site pages. They design sites so users can decide whether they want to dive deeper into the layers that interest them. Lai says, "It's a lot easier to create something complex than something simple and intuitive. Editing is an important part of the process."

In Search of Best Practices. When asked how the firm tests its navigation, the principals say they distrust the focus group approach, citing the Aeron chair and the Dyson vacuum as two examples of focus-group "failures" that went on to great success in the marketplace. They prefer testing with paper prototypes or creating quick Flash demos. They will test these with people who represent the target audience, and make revisions based on feedback.

"When clients ask us about best practices in the Web space, I remind them that our medium is less than ten years old," says Lai. "It's too young for us to cite any standards. It would stifle innovation. What people find 'intuitive' is still constantly evolving."

Lai goes on to add, "Good designers need to have an eye, not just visually, but for how things are experienced. We are continually investing in R&D. Good enough isn't enough—you have to be willing to go the extra mile."

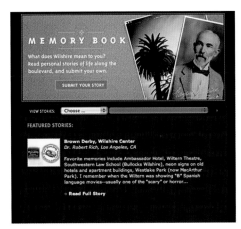

A "Memory Book" function allows visitors to contribute stories and photos about historic sites they've known and loved.

A menu bar at the bottom of the map provides a robust sorting functionality so users can "slice and dice" the detailed information according to their interests. You can look at buildings by date, function, style, architect, and preservation status.

Environmental Stewardship

Case Study
**Natural Resources
Defense Council**

Project
Website

Design Firm
Sullivan

The Natural Resources Defense Council (NRDC) is one of the most respected environmental organizations in the United States. With a focus on environmental law and the science that informs public policy, the organization works with committed scientists, environmental lawyers, and business experts to develop carefully considered, long-term, and pragmatic solutions to some of the world's most complex environmental issues.

Sullivan has been one of NRDC's strategic communications partners for many years. The firm helped NRDC create one of its earliest websites, and has continued to help them evolve their online presence. The goal has always been to project NRDC's expertise, and demonstrate the results the organization has achieved.

"We've learned how to help people find the information that's valuable to them."

—John Paolini

Helping Visitors Make Decisions. Sullivan's understanding of best practices from the for-profit world has been extremely helpful to NRDC. As John Paolini, Sullivan partner and executive creative director, points out, "With our work in the financial services sector, we're helping customers make big life decisions. We're helping them get a tangible picture of an invisible thing. So we've learned how to help people find the information that's valuable to them."

Targeted Approach. As NRDC's site has evolved, Sullivan has helped the organization strategize unique microsites. Sullivan talks about "pulling the graphic language" through this suite of sites that are designed to address specific audiences and initiatives. Rather than a completely centralized Web model, NRDC specifically promotes

its microsites in ads and newsletters, so diverse groups can quickly find the content they need.

Most recently, Sullivan helped NRDC develop a microsite targeted to builders, planners, architects, and developers of large-scale commercial and residential properties. The goal was to create a site that was a go-to destination for information, resources, and helpful tips about building green. NRDC wanted to make the process appealing enough that the audience would be interested to learn even more. The desired outcome was to communicate that building green is achievable, relatively simple, and potentially profitable.

Home

Build
Your
Business
Case

Set Your
Budget
and Goals

Adopt a
Whole-
Building
Approach

Apply
Sustainable
Building
Strategies

Capitalize
on Your
Achievement

Michael McWatters, Sullivan's creative director on the NRDC account, explains, "NRDC really wanted us to understand the needs and the dynamics of the builders and developers that would use the site." The teams at Sullivan have always used audience research to inform their strategic thinking. They regularly conduct user interviews when starting a project. McWatters says, "Quantitative research works well for transactional sites, but with sites that have a more emotional component, it's important to talk to people one-on-one."

Sullivan prepares a discussion guide for each interview. "We might ask some fairly abstract questions such as, 'If you're looking for information, what sources do you go to?' But we also drill down into specifics. You'd be amazed at how much you can tell about how a person likes to gather content when you can see how they organize their desks," he explains.

Strategic Stretch. As a nonprofit, NRDC does many of its site iterations with an in-house team using a content management system. But they continue to come

to Sullivan when they need to rethink the site, especially in light of best Web practices. Sullivan designer Andrea Stranger talks about how important it is to her to be able to work on nonprofit projects, especially with long-term clients: "The satisfaction of working with a nonprofit like NRDC is crucial to the whole Sullivan culture. It's even become an important draw for recruiting talent." She adds, "It's an opportunity for everyone to stretch their strategic muscles. Bottom line, we believe in it."

→ Sullivan helped NRDC develop a microsite targeted to builders, planners, architects, and developers of large-scale commercial and residential properties. The goal was to create a site that was an online, go-to destination for information, resources, and helpful tips about building green. Because the site's navigation is organized around the phases of the construction process, it reflects the way its audience thinks.

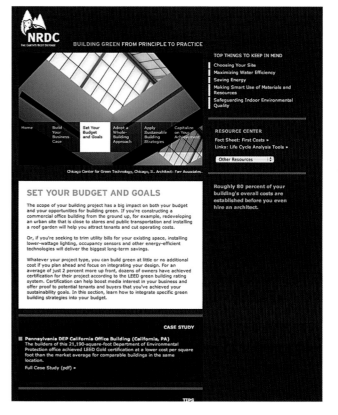

NRDC has struggled to showcase its many important initiatives and programs. An interactive scroll of graphic billboards provides display opportunities and allows users to access the issues they find particularly compelling. It also conveys a sense of vitality.

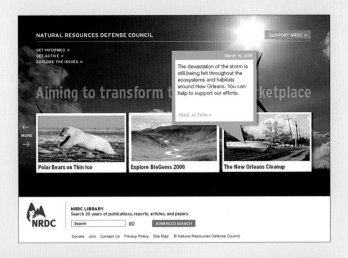

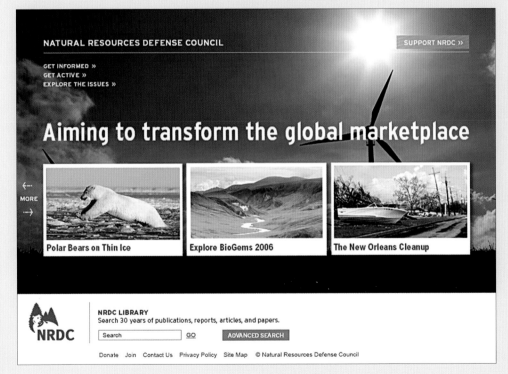

When Sullivan worked with NRDC on its most recent redesign, they learned in user interviews that there tended to be three types of visitors to the site: people in a learning mode (research), environmental news junkies, and those who wanted to take action. Based on this, the home page helps visitors navigate by way of three information "doorways."

Remembering the "Forgotten War"

Case Study
National WWI Museum

Project
Interactive Exhibits

Design Firm
**Second Story Interactive
Studios /Ralph Appelbaum
Associates**

For the National WWI Museum in Kansas City, Missouri, Second Story Interactive collaborated with exhibit lead designers Ralph Appelbaum Associates. The museum integrates objects, interactive technology, video, audio, animation, text, and graphics into media-based exhibits to give visitors a thought-provoking and participatory experience of World War I (WWI).

In addition to the most important study collection of WWI objects in the U.S., the museum includes the twelve plasma-screen Portrait Wall, two large Battlescape Maps, two 26-foot (7.9 m) Great War Tables, listening alcoves with historical audio recordings, plus a trench and a bomb crater visitors can walk into. Short films run at key moments of the exhibit to orient visitors and give them enough basic knowledge to fully understand the larger story of WWI.

"For museums, maximizing limited physical display space is tricky. The Web is a new gallery to publish content. Museums are exploring new ways to keep content on display and up to date. Interactive presentations put the museum's collection into greater context." —Josh Dudley

Interactive Tables. "Second Story excels at projects with deep content," explains Jennifer Young, Second Story producer. "The museum's two interactive tables weave together over 500 content elements showcasing deeper strategic and technical aspects of the war."

"At the beginning of our collaboration, Second Story realized there were too many permutations in the interactive content. The content was simplified as a natural part of the design process," says Josh Dudley, a designer at Ralph Appelbaum Associates.

The museum's tables require interactive pens. The technology allows different people to interact with the screen at the same time. "You can't do that with traditional touch screens," he continues. "And the table experience doesn't feel like an ATM machine."

Brad Johnson, creative director at Second Story, agrees. "If you do what museums did originally and put a bunch of computers everywhere, it looks like work."

Dudley notes, "Museums often rely on school groups. A table surface makes the activity social rather than a private act. You watch other people interact with available options, like being at a restaurant and seeing what they're ordering at the next table."

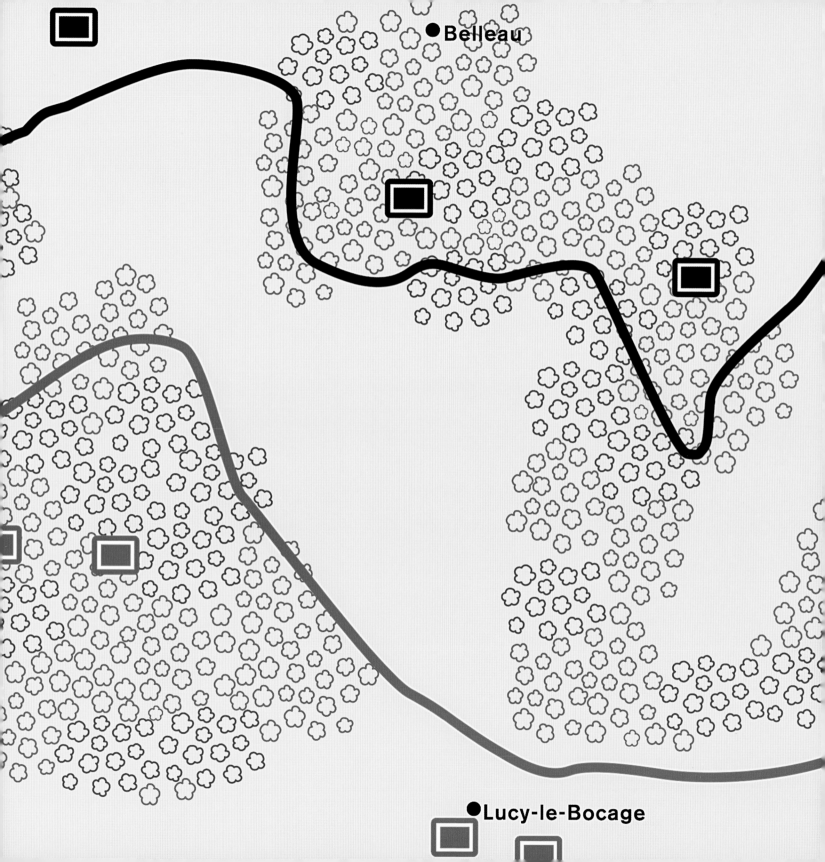

Creative Process and Collaboration.
"Second Story cares about what we care about: graphic look and feel, structure, and especially content. Second Story even hired their own historian to dialog with the museum's curator," explains Dudley.

"Our process is highly collaborative. We involve designers, programmers, and content producers at the early stages so everyone understands the story," Johnson says. "Collaborating with exhibit designers is exciting. We wanted to depart from a strictly screen-based experience to create unexpected environments that react to input from visitors."

Exhibit Design's Future. For museums, maximizing limited physical display space is tricky. The Web is a new gallery to publish content. Museums are exploring new ways to keep content on display and up to date.

"Interactive presentations put the museum's collection into greater context. People still come to a museum to see artifacts," says Young. "We integrate the best of both worlds. Visitors can view a single physical machine gun in the case and go to the interactive table to explore machine guns in greater detail."

The palette of options for exhibit design is expanding both on the technical and materials sides. "We like novel technologies, despite their risks, because surprise is memorable—it can help 'burn in' new information for visitors," says Dudley.

"These aren't theme park rides," he continues. "Museum visitors aren't constrained to a single pathway. They move through complex layered environments where the experience changes as you move through the space. You come to a museum to become more aware, and to be a better human being. It's best as a shared experience."

↑ In conjunction with large graphic panel installations, Battlescape Maps presented on touch screen monitors display the complexity of specific WWI battles.

↑ Visitors choose battles on a timeline and, through illustrations and accompanying narration, experience the distinctive and grueling nature of trench warfare as they watch battle lines shift and see territory lost and gained.

Second Story and Ralph Appelbaum Associates collaborated with Potion Design, the firm that created the technology for the tables. Visitors can experience the tables in two ways. In "individual mode," viewers sit at or walk around the table and select things that interest them. They can learn about military technology, view archival footage and photography, and create propaganda posters and email them. At any time, museum staff can launch the tables into a group-based interactive experience with up to twenty-four visitors engaging in a series of six "challenges" that illustrate different aspects of the war. Interstitial videos recap the experience between challenge sections.

Revitalizing a Brand

Case Study
Wilson Staff

Project
Website

Design Firm
VSA Partners

Ninety-year-old golf equipment brand Wilson Staff had lost its marketplace edge in the 1970s and wanted to gain it back. The company hired VSA Partners to re-execute the brand and give Wilson Staff the tools to continue its strategy in-house. During a year-long engagement, VSA Partners developed a comprehensive approach, including a new site that was launched in the U.S. and adopted by company branches in Europe, Canada, Japan, and Australia.

"The whole thing started with brand strategy," says VSA art director Jeff Walker. "Make Everyday Legendary" is the core concept and tagline for the campaign, which included a comprehensive relaunch of forty-two products across multiple media.

"There's a balance between the experiential and the more performance-oriented technical aspects of the site."

—Pat Heick

Integrated Look and Feel. The Wilson Staff brand has a rich visual legacy spanning over fifty years, including access to images of golf legends such as Sam Sneed and Gene Sarazen using their equipment. Like other brand materials, the website leverages this legacy to create a lifestyle experience of Wilson Staff while also satisfying a savvy golfer's need for deeper information about the product.

The look of the website was influenced by all the other branding VSA was doing. The interactive team took cues from Walker's designers across the aisle. "A lot of the website's style came from the print catalog, especially the layers of description," explains Pat Heick, VSA's director of interactive.

VSA's interactive team has eighteen members, including three information architects and usability experts. "We tried to take full advantage of the medium and make it very interactive," Heick says. "There's a balance between the experiential and the more performance-oriented technical aspects of the site."

Implementation and Launch. VSA implemented a legacy content management system (CMS) called Blue Martini. The site was developed in a CMS environment with developers and content managers. "We delivered design elements in layered

Photoshop format so that Wilson Staff can implement in-house updates that still look customized. Everything related to content management was very centralized for consistency," notes Heick.

VSA developed a three-part launch strategy for the website that was a marriage of the strategic and the practical.

"We liked the idea of having teasers to set up the relaunch, but also everything wasn't ready at once," explains Walker.

With Phase One, no product was shown. VSA instead played up lifestyle aspects of the game and asked the simple question: "Why golf?" Phase Two gave people glimpses of the reintroduced brand palette. "We didn't want to cannibalize the existing inventory, we just wanted to leak that new products were coming," says Walker. Phase Three's full launch showcased the print and PDF catalogs, and incorporated animations that spoke to the lifestyle, connectivity, and spirit of the game. When the full site went live, it also included a walk-through timeline depicting the history of the brand, deep product knowledge, and data sheets.

"What was great was that the plan we set out to execute was, in fact, the plan we did execute. We built momentum and Wilson really trusted us," says Heick.

"It was an amazing team effort," echoes Walker. "It was a fully integrated relaunch that worked well across every medium."

↑ In Phase One of the site, VSA played up lifestyle aspects of the game of golf instead of featuring product information.

The strong grid of the home page helps to orient the viewer. Visitors can select the type of information they are most interested in.

The text on all the product pages is organized into brief paragraphs and broken up with subheads for easy scanning. The bottom of every product page includes a display of related products.

Excavating Information

Case Study
National Institute for Research in Preventive Archaeology

Project
Intranet

Design Firm
Kahn + Associates

France's National Institute for Research in Preventive Archaeology (INRAP) is responsible for excavations throughout the country and its overseas territories, covering all periods from prehistory to modern day. The INRAP community includes 1,500 archaeologists located in France, as well as hundreds of support staff, governmental and scientific research partners, and contractors. Its mission is to disseminate and publish the results of its evaluations and excavations for the benefit of the research community and the general public.

When Kahn + Associates began to work with INRAP in 2006, the organization had already developed an extensive Internet site dedicated to informing the general public about its activities.

"Users stumbling across a particular topic of interest had no idea there was additional related content on the site and had no way to find it. Changing the architecture can fix that."

—Paul Kahn

New Intranet. The INRAP Intranet site needed improvement in order to gain greater user acceptance. "Our work with INRAP," explains K + A principal Paul Kahn, "involved several aspects of information architecture: improving the naming, classification, and organization of both sites, integrating current and new resources into a scientific portal, and helping to define the tasks and schedule needed to attain these goals."

Creating the Information Architecture.
K + A began by analyzing the information architecture of the intranet and producing an isometric (dimensional) diagram of the existing site.

For the next stage of the project, K + A developed user scenarios to illustrate how information was presented and linked on the Internet and intranet sites. They reused the isometric diagrams created earlier, adding an overlay of information related to the scenario.

The new diagram showed how information related to a single subject (such as all the excavations in the city of Nîmes) was actually housed across several different sections of the Internet and intranet sites, and was often not accessible via navigation links on the site. "Users stumbling across a particular topic of interest had no idea there was additional related content on the site and had no way to find it," explains Kahn. "Changing the architecture can fix that."

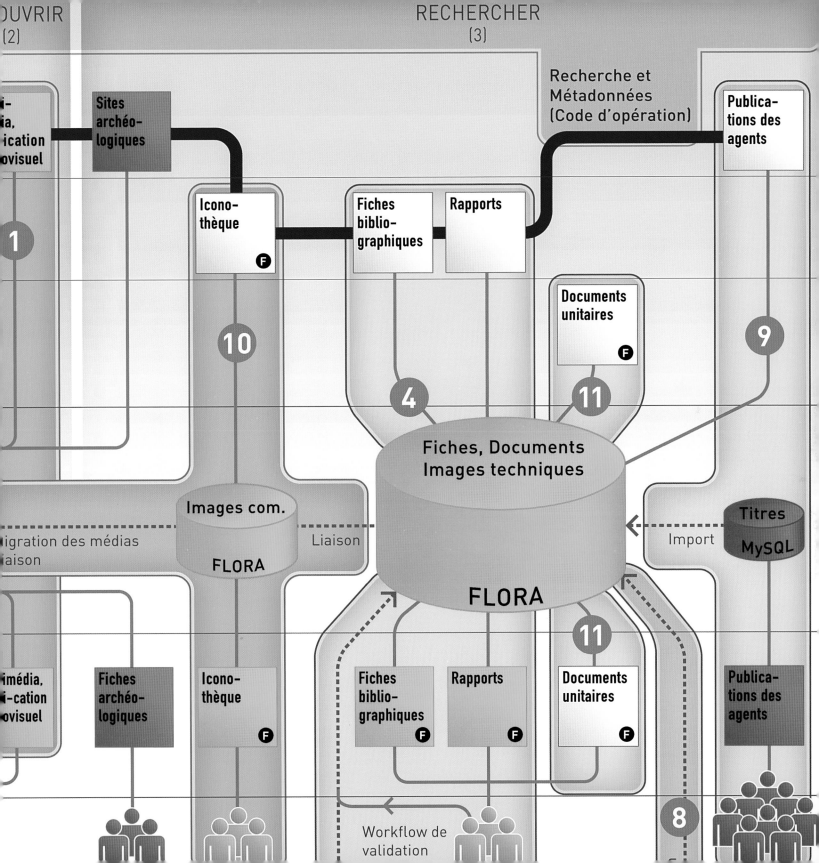

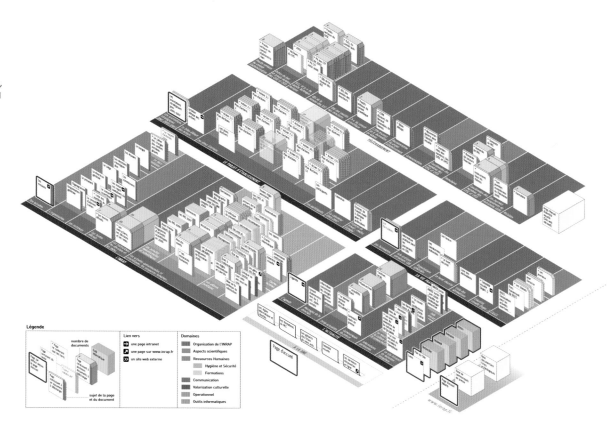

→ With this isometric (dimensional) diagram, designers Laurent Kling and Eva-Lotta Lamm of K + A described the current organization of the site content, then used color coding as visual cues for the redistribution of the content within a new naming structure.

"We finally recommended developing the scientific portal not as a separate site but as the professional view of the reorganized INRAP Internet site," says Kahn. The site was organized around four sections: Inform, Discover, Search, and Participate. To illustrate this transformation, K + A developed a series of wireframes. (For further explanation about wireframes, see Chapter 3.)

Dimensional Diagramming. An isometric map offers advantages for addressing two problems that information designers often face when mapping any network or large site: 1) minimizing the lines that represent links between pages and 2) representing large numbers of elements in a single map.

By using the z-dimension (depth) in combination with "floor" patterns and color, the arrangement of one page behind another implies a navigational connection, without turning the map into a wiring diagram. The position of the pages or boxes on the z-axis allows for overlap of many elements while still providing a surface for labeling the page. This allows for representation of many more elements on the diagram.

Designing around the Architecture.
Once K + A's information architecture recommendations were reviewed and accepted, they delivered a complete set of page-level wireframes to LM communiquer, the design agency responsible for INRAP's visual identity. LM communiquer used the wireframes as a blueprint while they developed the look and feel for the site.

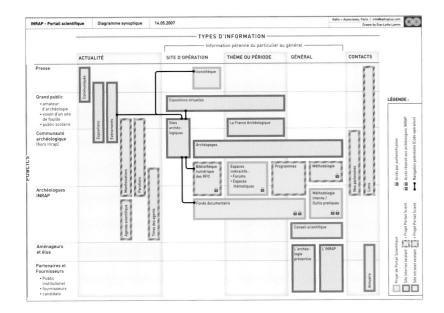

To facilitate discussion between the different stakeholders, K + A developed a summary diagram to show each of the information collections. Information is arranged according to audience type and information type. Color was added to differentiate between the existing Internet and intranet, and the proposed scientific portal.

Like most wireframes, these made no reference to actual visual design, but instead showed the general positioning of information on the page. This wireframe shows the scientifically oriented content available to archaeologists who have logged onto the site.

The synoptic diagram presents K + A's conclusions about the structure of the site. The horizontal axis of the diagram represents the four sections of the site. The vertical axis shows the depth of the project process, including editorial systems, database applications, personnel, and information sources.

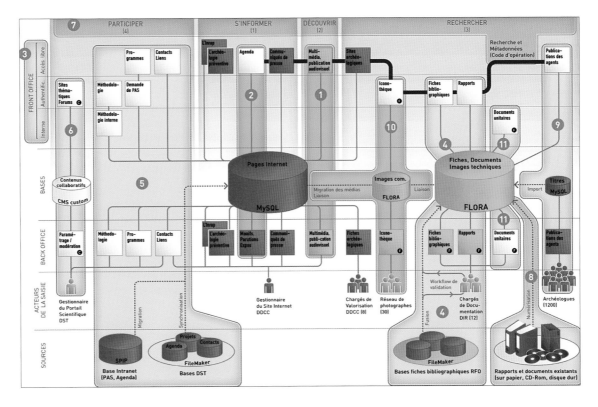

Speedy Cuisine

Case Study
TurboChef

Project
Device Interface

Design Firm
frog design

Want to cook a rack of lamb in eight minutes? An entire turkey in just forty-two? TurboChef's Speedcook technology had been used in commercial kitchens for over a decade. Known for product innovation, frog design signed on to design a product delivering the same professional cooking experience to the home. "Not every oven is just an oven," suggests frog creative director Jennifer Kilian. The idea that things aren't exactly what they seem often characterizes frog's work. The studio's most distinctive projects merge industrial design with digital and interactive design. The trick lies in making sure that physical design, visual design, and technology work together seamlessly—and that simplicity and intuition rule.

> "To emotionally engage users in the product, we needed to learn three levels of user needs: stated needs, observed needs, and latent (unstated) needs."
>
> —Jennifer Kilian

Not Just an Oven. The Speedcook's features include its cookwheel, an interactive touch screen with a cooking wizard, the ability to add meals to a favorites list, and more. "The biggest design challenge was shifting the user's thinking process from a traditional time-and-temperature paradigm into something that uses algorithms and a wizard," explains Kilian.

The screen-based wizard's set of pathways guides users through a complex set of choices while allowing them to feel in control. There's a vast food encyclopedia built into the software, which lets users turn the cookwheel knob to select a variety of functions and narrow down choices. If a user selects "roast," the screen wizard prompts for more specifics, asking, "Poultry or beef?" If poultry is selected, the wizard asks, "Turkey or chicken?" then, "Whole or stuffed?" to complete the process and ensure the correct cooking time.

Emotional Approach. The frog team begins projects with solid research. Their unique approach focuses on the emotion of the experience. Kilian explains, "Our founder, Hartmut Esslinger, says, 'Product sells, but emotion buys.'"

Baby boomers comprise a good portion of TurboChef's target residential market. The frog team identified three specific user groups: "foodies" who love buying ovens; "wannabes" who like the idea of cooking but want to spend more time with family; and "homies" who spend lots of time at home but don't spend as much on ovens or eating out.

The frog team spent hours hanging out in people's kitchens. "To emotionally engage users in the product, we needed to learn three levels of user needs: stated needs, observed needs, and latent (unstated) needs," Kilian continues. "Finding latent needs is like dusting for fingerprints—you know they're there, but finding them is a challenge."

They uncovered users' feelings about the idea of such an oven. Would it make life easier? Did it harken back to simpler times? Would it inspire creativity? The frog team noted the objects in people's kitchens.

"We saw things like Grandma's teapot, completely nostalgic, next to a laptop where the home chef was finding recipes online," explains Kilian.

Design Approach: Hearth and Home.
The designers wanted to emphasize the sense of nostalgia, heritage, and hearth they found in people's kitchens. "Warm colors, especially on our 'hero' product design with the orange-brown oven door, recall a time when baby boomers were growing up," explains Kilian.

There was strong interplay between the project's physical design, information design, typography, color, and graphical look and feel. "We considered how a set of colors would influence emotion. Oranges and reds help users connect with appetite, home, and hearth, with blue as an accent color," says Kilian.

"When we tested the product model/prototype in our studio, we asked users what they thought it was and what it might do," notes Kilian. "People knew, at a glance, there was something different about the upper oven. Because of the extra curve, the beautiful handle, and the door color, they could tell it was something special."

The physical product designers at frog debated on whether to use a digital or analog clock. Information and visual designers working on the settings prototypes had featured analog-feeling informational graphics in their screen designs, which helped drive the decision to use an analog clock on the oven.

The Speedcook oven has a vast food encyclopedia built into the software, which lets users turn the cookwheel knob to select a variety of functions and narrow down choices.

Designers wanted to ensure that the product was intuitive and that nontechnical users were confident enough to use it. "We asked product testers to pretend to roast a turkey. They'd turn the knob. By the second or third screen they figured it out and were thrilled," says frog's Jennifer Kilian.

Where do you need to go, how do you find it, what do you do when you get there? Signage and wayfinding ensure that people aren't in a perpetual state of disorientation in the world at large. With exhibit design, information becomes theater. Successful environmental design takes substantial amounts of information, shapes a story, and determines the best ways to engage with audiences as they move through a space.

ENVIRONMENTAL CASE STUDIES

→ **Metro Design Studio**

→ **Hunt Design**

→ **Bureau Mijksenaar**

→ **Durfee Regn Sandhaus**

→ **Poulin + Morris**

→ **Infinite Scale Design Group**

Learning to Love Public Transport

Case Study
Los Angeles County Metropolitan Transportation Authority

Project
Metro LA Signage Guidelines

Design Firm
Metro Design Studio

The City of Los Angeles is notorious for its cars, freeways, and dearth of public transportation. The Metropolitan Transportation Authority (Metro) is the public agency that manages the city's buses and trains. For many years, public perception of the transportation system and the agency that runs it was extremely jaded. But along with changes at the top levels of management came a sophisticated appreciation for the role design plays in communicating information, creating good customer experiences, and fostering good will.

Creative director Michael Lejeune was hired to rethink the whole internal marketing and design department. Neil Sadler, formerly with MetaDesign, joined the team as senior designer.

"Templates provide a structure to help people organize information. You're saying, 'Don't change the font. Think about the message instead.'" —Neil Sadler

Where to Begin? When Sadler and Lejeune first started at Metro, it seemed as if every project they approached was like turning a stone over and finding another twenty projects that needed to be tackled. Metro was using twelve to fifteen logos at the time, and the signage system employed wildly inconsistent fonts and icons. There were huge numbers of ad hoc, homemade signs.

Sadler and Lejeune knew that effective guidelines would include different parts that would be useful to different audiences. Outside consultants and design firms would use the standards to help implement signage projects. Consultants would even be able to use the guidelines as part of the initial bidding process. The guidelines would also help internal departments, especially if the document was posted to the intranet.

Because there were such diverse audiences, the guidelines would have to cover some very fundamental information—even addressing such topics as "What is a font?"

Decision Points. Once they had produced the standards, the design department was able to have clearer conversations with people in the field to find out what was really needed. A 3-D rendering helped address questions about "decision points" for signage. Sadler says, "You have to put yourself in your mother's shoes. You have to ask yourself, 'At which point will she have a question? And what question will she have?'"

FINANCIAL DISTRICT

JEWELRY DISTRICT

Wilshire Grand Hotel & Center

Old Fire Sta. No. 28

Fine Arts Building

818 Building

7th St/Metro Center Station

700 South Flower Building

Post Office

Hyatt Regency Los Angeles

Macy's Plaza (MCI Center)

Chase Plaza

Embassy Hotel &

Roosevelt Building

Old Robinsons Building

Gardens California Club

The Standard Hotel

AON Center

Richard J. Riordan Central Library

AT&T Center

Hilton Check

One Wilshire Building

Oviatt Building

Giannini Plaza

Pacific Center

Brock Jewelers Building

Los Angeles Athletic Club

WILSHIRE

HOPE

GRAND

FLOWER

6TH

7TH

8TH

ST

BL

ST

ST

Plaza

A	Metro Local Bus Stop
⊙ **A**	Metro Rapid Bus Stop
⌖	Metro Rail Station Entrance
▭	Metro Rail Station
▬	Metro Red Line
▬	Metro Purple Line

And then 'How can I get her the right information?'" One of the most valuable pages in the guidelines asks the fundamental question: "Do you really need a sign? And if you do, what kind of sign is it? What is the primary message, the secondary message?"

Templates Save the Day. Sadler goes on to say, "The real promise of guidelines is to help people work with templates—you focus people on filling things in. Templates

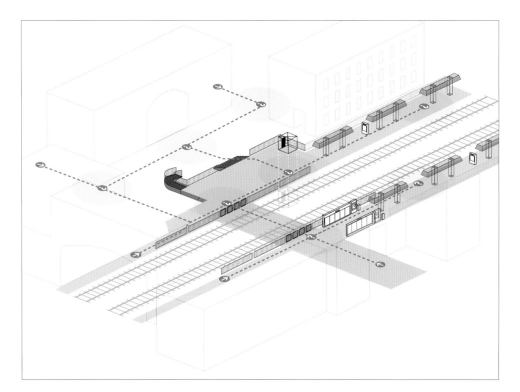

In planning signage, the sequence in which the viewer will encounter the information is key. The goal is to have all stations develop and display signage in a consistent, clear manner from the street level to the platform area, to create a seamless experience as travelers move from station to station.

Smart copywriting, a lively color palette, and careful type styling are employed in the design of a user-friendly ticket booth.

provide a structure to help people organize information. You're saying, 'Don't change the font. Think about the message instead.'"

The Need to Iterate. Sadler came to realize that the process of creating standards works best by tackling a situation, fixing it, and then documenting it. "The best guidelines come from a project you've successfully completed. You stand back and say, 'Well, that worked, but this didn't.'" He observes, "It's essentially a never-finished document.

And there are always exceptions that have to be addressed."

There Are Rewards. Sadler observes, "You have to get the right people in the room to find out how they actually do their jobs and what the problems are. If you listen to their input, they'll understand you're trying to make their jobs easier, not harder. You can actually create a pride of ownership. The reason I took this job is because I can do things that matter."

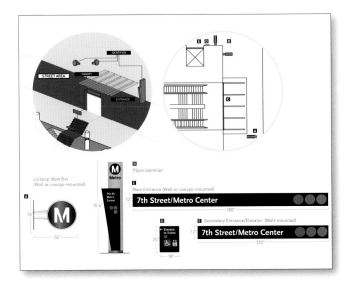

The design team consulted the operations crews ultimately responsible for installing signs. Based on these discussions, the designers created guidelines to address often overlooked issues. Station workers now feel a pride of ownership in the system.

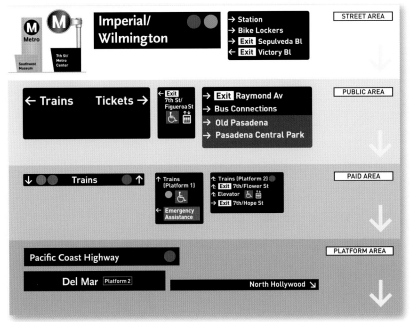

Metro's standards include typographic guidelines for the progression of information as travelers pass through the station. The system is designed so the information becomes more specific as travelers get closer to the platform.

Navigating Alcatraz

Case Study
**Golden Gate National
Parks Conservancy**

Project
Signage and Master Plan

Design Firm
Hunt Design

Hunt Design specializes in graphic design for buildings, spaces, and places. As an extension of the firm's ongoing work in developing signage guidelines for California's extensive Golden Gate Recreation Area, the firm has created a signage program for Alcatraz Island. San Francisco's number one tourist destination, this historically significant island draws multigenerational audiences from around the world.

Alcatraz served as a military fortification in the 1850s and an incarceration facility for Spanish-American War prisoners. It is notorious for its role as a federal maximum-security prison from 1934 to 1963. American Indians seized and occupied Alcatraz from 1969 to 1971 in a successful protest against the United States' Bureau of Indian Affairs. The island is now a nature preserve.

"It's important that the interpretive signs are of interest to all age levels. This is a medium to get the party started."

—Wayne Hunt

What's around That Corner? Hunt Design began the wayfinding aspect of the Alcatraz project with a site and information plan. Principal Wayne Hunt explains, "At the most basic, we know we need to put messages where people need to find them: at dead ends, turns, and intersections. Alcatraz is quite linear in how you're first allowed to see it, but then it opens up to a loose circulation approach that is more like a theme park model. When you design for theme parks, you learn to always give the viewer something to look for to pull them through the space."

Tapestry of Stories. In addition to the wayfinding system, Hunt Design created interpretive graphics to help visitors explore the island's many features. Hunt says his firm is most excited about projects that combine aspects of both wayfinding and exhibits "where you're part of making the place and explaining it too." He says signage systems can be colorful and more complex when they're about placemaking. This is in contrast to an environment like a hospital, where the wayfinding has to emphasize simple functionality.

But even when a place is a vacation destination, Hunt Design knows people can only absorb so much information. Hunt says, "You need to design for streakers, strollers, and studiers. We know a good exhibit will let a visitor jog through and learn something. But we also want someone to be able to stay for three hours and still be intrigued."

Hunt Design is most excited about projects that combine aspects of both wayfinding and exhibits "where you're part of making the place and explaining it too," says Hunt.

The firm employs many of the same principles used to design magazines for flip-through readers. Hunt says, "By the third sentence, you lose people. If we can feature a really interesting image with an intriguing headline, we'll get people to slow down. You need short, crisp declarative writing."

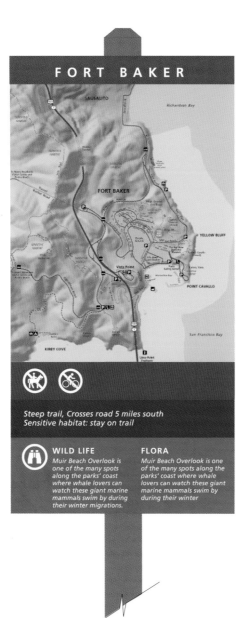

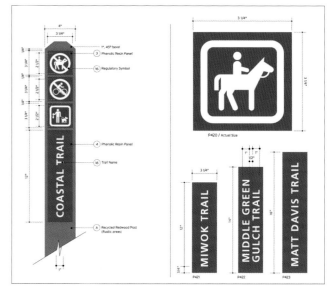

In addition to narrative signage, the master plan called for wayfinding signs for vehicular traffic and pedestrian trails.

"Suggestions we've made for headlines in initial mock-ups will often end up being part of the final installation. After doing this for years, we've learned how to help clients shape their content into distinct parts and chapters." —Wayne Hunt

Opportunities for Interaction. Hunt Design has found that interpretive signs can help stimulate interaction—between guests, parents and kids, or staff and the public. So it's important that the interpretive signs are of interest to all age levels. As Hunt sums it up, "This is a medium to get the party started."

Hunt talks about the future of the "smart visit," where people will be able to visit a destination and get customized information as they walk through exhibits, or get information about how they can go online and learn even more. He offers, "There's always going to be a limit to what people will be able to absorb in a forty-minute visit. But maybe we can get you excited and wanting more."

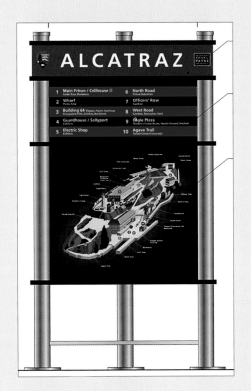

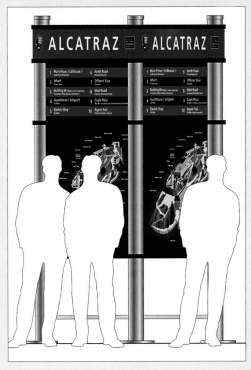

↑ "You need to design for streakers, strollers, and studiers. We know a good exhibit will let a visitor jog through and learn something. But we also want someone to be able to stay for three hours and still be intrigued," says Hunt.

Signage to the Rescue

Case Study
Various

Project
Transportation Graphics

Design Firm
Bureau Mijksenaar

Traveling can be incredibly stressful. In fact, many people have recurring nightmares of racing to catch a plane while carrying huge amounts of luggage. But most travelers will attest that in real life, good wayfinding signage can make all the difference.

Meet Paul Mijksenaar, the founder and director of the highly respected Bureau Mijksenaar. Based in Amsterdam, with an office in New York, Mijksenaar is a specialist in creating visual information systems, such as signage systems for railway stations and airports around the world. At the beginning of every project, Bureau Mijksenaar begins by asking questions and uncovering information about how travelers experience the travel environment in question.

> **"As a designer, you have to think in time and see things in sequence. You have to see information as a narrative form."**
>
> —Paul Mijksenaar

Ask at the Information Booth. "When we start a new project, we always start by asking for the customer satisfaction surveys," Mijksenaar says. "Larger organizations have this data because they continually survey. At the very least, we will talk to the customer service representatives, or the folks who work at the information booth. We try to determine the ten questions visitors most often ask. This will indicate the main problems with the current system."

The Big Picture. "As a designer, you have to think in time and see things in sequence. You have to see information as a narrative form. This is true whether you're designing signage for an airport or a form to be used by the post office. But people need to have a sense of overview first; they want to get a feeling for what is going on, for what will happen at the end, before they drill down into the sequence. Good teachers have always known this," Mijksenaar says.

In addition to a good sense of sequence, Mijksenaar believes effective information designers have to know how to build a bit of tension. He invokes the way Hitchcock directed his films. "You have to build up information to keep people's interest so they stay attentive."

Going Down the Wrong Path. Mijksenaar speaks passionately about some misconceptions people have about using pictograms

 Wayfinding signage in this terminal at New York City's JFK International Airport provides clear information for travelers.

in public spaces. He says designers expect them to be self-explanatory. Mijksenaar believes icons can be handy tools to reinforce things people already understand, but he points out if you don't know what an ATM is, it won't do you any good to see an icon for one. He says this is particularly important in environments such as hospitals, where people are often clueless about what they're trying to find.

The Wild World of Color. Mijksenaar has recently been rethinking the role that color plays in his work. "Color is one of the most powerful design tools we have. It attracts the most attention. But it has limitations.

People can't recall more than seven colors at a time, so this can be a problem in assigning hierarchies and meaning," he explains. "And the problem is that designers will often use color to simultaneously convey different things. Sometimes it's about aesthetics, or branding, or to establish categories. Because people have experienced color in a confusing way, they will often ignore it. So my approach has been to only use color if there's a need for it. We work from the bottom up when we map the information, and in the past, I would always recommend using scale to convey hierarchy."

All maps at the Schiphol Airport in Amsterdam are oriented according to the viewer's perspective: Destinations that appear on the left side of the map can be found to the viewer's left, and destinations at the top of the map can be found straight ahead of the viewer. On the reverse side of this directory, the whole map is mirrored.

The color coding system at Schiphol Airport uses basic color categories: yellow for flight information, black for airport services, blue for retail and food.

But Mijksenaar has softened his stand on color in the last couple of years. "I've come to realize that some of my hesitance to use color was actually a conflict in myself. I was trained as an information architect. Instead of thinking of how to make things attractive, I was trained to think only of hierarchies of information. I like gray. But after twenty-five years of doing this, I've realized that people love color, and that in addition to providing information, providing satisfaction is a function in itself." He adds, "This work is rewarding because you actually get feedback from the users. People will tell us, 'Now we can find our way!'"

This airport has a color coded signing system

Follow yellow signs when flying	Follow black signs for airport services	Follow green signs when leaving the airport
• Ticketing • Arrivals • Gates • Check-in	• Restrooms • Phones • Escalators	• Ground Transportation • Parking

↑ This courtesy sign explains the airport's color coded signage system. The same system applies to all three airports of the Port Authority of New York, as well as to the Newark Airport in New Jersey.

↑ All airport signs related to ground transportation at JFK are color coded green to match U.S. highway signage. Mijksenaar also edited the airport nomenclature to achieve a comprehensive and consistent message system.

↑ Signs at the Departures Lounge of Terminal 4 at JFK

Envisioning the Wide Open West

Case Study
**The Huntington Library
and Botanical Gardens**

Project
Exhibit Design

Design Firm
Durfee Regn Sandhaus

The Great Wide Open, an exhibition organized by The Huntington Library and Botanical Gardens, was focused on a single medium, the panoramic photograph, as it has documented the American West from the 1850s to the present.

With a width-to-height ratio of two-to-one (and often substantially more), a panoramic photograph can show much more than a conventional photograph, and is ideally suited to the pictorial demands of the West's epic dimensions.

The design firm for the exhibition was Durfee Regn Sandhaus (DRS), a Los Angeles-based collaboration of the architecture studio Durfee|Regn and the communications design studio Louise Sandhaus Design (LSD). The three principals have a long history of collaborating on complex interdisciplinary projects, including museum exhibitions.

> **"This isn't a book, it's a physical experience. There are other strategies to use, other ways to communicate the curators' ideas."**
>
> —Louise Sandhaus

It's All About the Experience. Sandhaus says, "I've never thought of myself as an exhibition designer. It doesn't matter if the project is a book, on-screen, or an environment—it's all about information design for me." Sandhaus recalls a long-ago stint working on a graphic interface for software. "In order to solve the problem, I created some storyboard scenarios for the experience and I realized it was all about how someone would navigate the space. This forever changed my design process."

What Are You Communicating? As the trio maps out an exhibition approach, they know that people will navigate the space in a variety of ways, so they can't design a linear narrative. But they also understand that people need some orientation to the exhibition's ideas. "When we meet with clients we try to help them reframe the design of the exhibition as a communication problem to be solved," Sandhaus says. "This can be an unusual approach for curators. We ask, 'What are you trying to communicate, and how can this happen in a sophisticated way?'"

Sandhaus explains, "There will always be visitors that move quickly through an exhibition. You feature certain things so they'll walk out and be able to tell someone about it. And you hope they leave thinking about what they've seen. But you also design another level that goes deeper."

"Just as the invention of the printing press meant public documents could be exchanged and debated, I think of my work as invoking the intelligence of the visual." —Louise Sandhaus

↑ The exhibition explored spatial metaphors as organizing principles. Five thematic sections— Range, Pathway, Grid, Site, and Tribe—were used to classify the ideas and materials of the exhibition to suggest the panorama's representation of time and space, as well as its narrative qualities.

→ At the entrance of this exhibition, a wide-angle window allowed visitors to see the gallery in a panoramic way. Wide-angle view- finders embedded in the window created additional panoramic experiences. Looking through the lens, a small title for each thematic section appeared super- imposed over its corresponding location in the space.

"When I see a lot of text on the walls at an exhibition that is difficult to read while standing, I'm thinking, 'This isn't a book, it's a physical experience. There are other strategies to use, other ways to communicate the curators' ideas.'"

Creating a Dialog. The partners say their brainstorming sessions create the magic. They bring in objects, and other visual references that inspire them, even if they are things that might feel tangential. And then they start sketching, and asking, "What about this? Would this be possible?"

"When we begin a project, we don't split our roles. We're all involved in the conceptualization. It's all integrated," Sandhaus explains. "But at a certain point Tim [Durfee] deals with the architectural issues, I address the graphics, and Iris [Regn] has a great eye for details such as furnishings that ultimately finesse the show."

For this exhibit, DRS sought to create a gallery environment that appeared open and boundless, to mimic the feeling of open space found in the photographs. "We had to get rid of the walls. We needed people to have a close view, a medium view, and a long view," Sandhaus says.

"My interest is in helping people share common knowledge in order to start a dialog. I'm interested in how exhibitions can do this. Just as the invention of the printing press meant public documents could be exchanged and debated, I think of my work as invoking the intelligence of the visual," Sandhaus says.

 The logo treatment for the exhibition reinforced the panoramic theme.

The large platform-like surfaces that were designed to create paths of circulation abstractly referred to landscape features, and allowed visitors to get both long and close views of the photographs.

Paying Tribute

Case Study
**World Trade Center
Visitor Center**

Project
Exhibit Design

Design Firm
Poulin + Morris

Poulin + Morris' offices are fifteen blocks from the site of the World Trade Center (WTC) buildings. But it's not just physical proximity that made the firm a good candidate for designing the tribute museum for the two iconic buildings. Located less than 50 feet (15 m) from Ground Zero, the museum's mission, defined by the September 11th Families' Association, is to transmit the voices of the 9/11 community: victims' families, rescue workers, attack survivors, volunteers—everyone touched by the total destruction of the site on September 11, 2001.

The goal: Create a world-class experience that would commemorate, inform, and convey the whole story, including the history of the WTC and the role it had played in the community.

"A project like this requires a complex team. We collaborated with BKSK Architects, an educational specialist, an archivist, a lighting specialist, and audiovisual experts. The whole team has to agree to a singular goal. You have to respect each other's strengths."

—Richard Poulin

Diverse Audience. Poulin + Morris needed to make sure the WTC Visitor Center would appeal to a broad audience. Ground Zero is a major tourist destination for people from around the world, and local school groups would be frequent visitors. Because of these diverse audiences, Poulin + Morris wanted to focus on an image-based story. They also knew that layering information could help different audiences with levels of expertise find a way to relate to the material.

The Center's director of education, who took on the role of curator, created an outline and gathered great quantities of artifacts, photos, videos, and remnants. The amount of photography and news footage gathered was extraordinary. Whether taken by professionals or witnesses, the images conveyed a story that was primal and immediate. Poulin + Morris' task was to help edit and structure the narrative.

The Difference a Day Makes. In thinking how to best convey the gravity of the actual disaster, it seemed logical to use time—in fact, twenty-four hours—as the organizing principle. On September 11th so much had happened so fast, and everyone had experienced the events in such a surreal way.

"Normally, when one works on an exhibit, one is trying to create an overarching narrative, something a larger group of people can understand. But with projects like this, people are terrified of losing their individual stories. It's critical not to homogenize or generalize. That's the challenge." —Richard Poulin

⬆ A series of floor-to-ceiling time-line units invite visitors to travel a 40-foot (12.2 m)-long corridor and actually walk through the events of both February 26, 1993 (a previous bomb attack on the WTC) and September 11, 2001. As visitors move through these individual "person-to-person histories," they become part of conversations with multiple perspectives.

⬆ Images, audio, video, and a glowing 8-foot (2.4 m)-high model of the World Trade Center towers interactively orient visitors to the WTC community. A giant floor map orients the visitor geographically, showing where the WTC fit into the surrounding area.

Floor-to-ceiling acrylic fins were designed to tell the story by time increments, marking the events of the day as they happened.

Richard Poulin says most New Yorkers remember how extraordinarily blue the sky was the morning of 9/11. In one of the most moving parts of the exhibition, a mural that begins as an expanse of blue, just like the sky that day, gradually fills with missing-person posters, stretching from floor to ceiling at the far end of the gallery. This collage invokes the iconic image of walls all over lower Manhattan covered with posters for weeks after the disaster, as families looked for their missing loved ones.

The Nature of a Memorial. Because the client was an affiliation that included families, the NYC Police and Fire Departments, and others, working to satisfy so many viewpoints added complexity to the project.

Poulin recalls the experience he had many years ago working on the interpretive planning for the Holocaust Museum in Washington, D.C., and how it helped prepare him for the WTC project. "It taught me so much about human behavior. It taught me how to work with emotionally charged stories, where the subjective point of view is so important. Normally, when one works on an exhibit, one is trying to create an overarching narrative, something a larger group of people can understand. But with projects like this, people are terrified of losing their individual stories. It's critical not to homogenize or generalize. That's the challenge," Poulin says.

↑ A timeline display gives the history of the WTC. Like a family album, with pictures of birthday parties and other significant events, the photos came from people who had worked in the towers. Photomurals in the background show the vantage point from the observation deck of one of the towers.

↑ A contemplative gallery, in which the names of all victims are inscribed in glass and projected on a wall, houses mementoes, keepsakes, and tributes sent by victim's relatives. The intent was to give each and every family the chance to tell their own story.

Celebrating Athletic Excellence

Case Study
**Brigham Young
University**

Project
Exhibit Design

Design Firm
Infinite Scale Design Group

Brigham Young University (BYU) has a long-standing and emotional connection to its athletic traditions. Its new 10,000-square-foot (929 sq. m) Student Athlete Center was designed to include a three-level athletic hall of fame celebrating 100 years of BYU athletics across a wide spectrum of sports. The goal was to appeal to alumni, former athletes and their families, prospective athletes the university recruits, and the scores of current BYU athletes passing through the light-filled atrium to the training rooms each day.

Many firms around the world specialize in the design of athletic halls, but Infinite Scale Design Group's principals had produced the impressive graphics for the Winter Olympic Games in Salt Lake City, and the firm's passion for all things athletic got them the job.

"We were looking to create a story that was connective and cohesive, and we wanted to steer clear of the overstuffed attic approach common to so many athletic halls." —Cameron Smith

Knowing What You Have. When Infinite Scale was hired, building construction had just begun. One of the first tasks was to sort through copious amounts of memorabilia—all saved lovingly but randomly in closets, dusty trophy cases, and file cabinets. Infinite Scale helped BYU develop a web-based content management system for tracking every artifact so they could document the location, ownership, and condition of each item in the collection.

From their evaluation of the content and the space, and after many sit-down sessions with the clients and architects, Infinite Scale mapped out the content they needed to represent. They calculated how much floor and wall space could be allocated to each sport, and how to prioritize the space based on who would be using it and what they would want to see. Infinite Scale's team remembers how the plan evolved as it went through several iterations.

"We were looking to create a story that was connective and cohesive, and we wanted to steer clear of the overstuffed attic approach common to so many athletic halls," says partner Cameron Smith, the firm's creative director.

More Trophies to Come. One of the biggest challenges was how to plan for future growth. The school plans to win trophies for years to come, so every aspect of the exhibition was designed for expansion—

including memorabilia cases, timelines, and photo walls. Infinite Scale needed to configure the space and the graphic approach so the exhibition would look fantastic upon opening, but so that BYU could also continue to add to it as time went on. The firm developed a "kit of parts," and a style guide with guidelines for pictograms, color, typography, and materials.

These guidelines were also used to coordinate with the interactive firm that worked on the screen-based parts of the exhibition, so the interface would be tied to the rest of the exhibition. Interactive displays would make a tremendous amount of information available to visitors, without making the exhibit itself overly cluttered. The additional information wasn't visible unless the visitor wanted to drill down for more details on a particular event or athlete.

A Living, Breathing Space. In contrast to a traditional museum space where every visitor has chosen to spend time with an exhibition, the three-story atrium is, as Infinite Scale partner Amy Lukas describes it, "a living space." People work and travel through the area all day long. Because of this, the sound requirements of the exhibition were particularly important to address.

Smith worked with the architects to source spherical dome speakers that would allow visitors to easily hear interactive content when standing within a 10-foot (3-m) radius, but where the sound wouldn't encroach on the other spaces. The lighting requirements were equally as important to manage to ensure displays were perfectly legible.

In the end, Infinite Scale feels that timing is one of the most important factors for success with an exhibition design project. The partners note, "When we work with clients, we strongly encourage them to get us on board as early as possible. It saves money and gives us the chance to make the project even better."

↑ Every aspect of the exhibition needed to accommodate future growth—memorabilia cases, timelines, and photo walls.

↑ The display system allows BYU to continue to add elements.

What can we learn when we use design techniques or new technology to reveal new patterns of information? Designers are constantly pushing the envelope to invent new ways of presenting ideas. The ultimate goal: creative expression, exploration, and new connections. The following interviews address the creators' intentions for these experimental projects.

EXPERIMENTAL CASE STUDIES

→ **World Filter Visualization**

→ **Digg Labs**

→ **Chris Jordan**

→ **Similar Diversity**

→ **We Feel Fine and Yahoo! Time Capsule**

→ **Wikipedia Activity**

World Filter Visualization

Design Firm
Information Design Studio

Project
Interactive Map

Q&A with
Gerlinde Schuller, Principal

With so many opportunities for networking, using the Web can still feel like a lonely, anonymous experience. We may suspect that our behavior is being tracked online, but we almost never get to see the digital traces or footprints we leave as we explore. The Netherlands-based design firm, Information Design Studio, developed this World Filter as a way to connect with site visitors and to engage their participation in mapping a unique view of the world.

"**Users leave a visual trace on our website, and can watch the traces of other people around the world. It is like moving your finger on a globe and imagining a world trip.**"

—Gerlinde Schuller

What inspired the name "The World as Flatland"? Can you explain the World Filter?

GS: We named our website "The World as Flatland" because we see that as a metaphor for information design: translating large amounts of data into flat, two-dimensional form. We developed the World Filter for the home page to show a surprising visualization of statistical website data.

Visitors are located via their Internet protocol (IP) number on a map of the world. By visiting our website, they add their country to the overview of the world, thus further completing it. People are surprised that they are located and that they get a personal welcome-greeting (e.g., *"Ciao Italia"*) on a design website.

How did you determine the criteria by which your users can "filter the world"?

GS: The assembly of the world map depends on the visitor's decision to enter the site. If our database can locate a site visitor by IP, their city name and country's shape appears; otherwise they are counted as "unknowns." Another filter offers different world statistics of potential collective interest, such as "Where do people live longest in the world?"

India
18 visitors

4 Bangalore   1 Pune
3 Lucknow   5 Unknown City
1 Ahmedabad
1 Ara
1 Delhi
1 Mahâlandi
1 Mumbai

Filter the world
I am happy
I am beautiful
I am a genius
I am spoiled
I love my country
I am speechless
I leave my country
I will live long

Filter the world ▼

The World as Flatland's "World Filter" is a visual interpretation of Web and world statistics. Visitors are located via their IP number on a map of the world. By visiting the website, visitors add their country to the overview of the world.

Censored Countries

The 10 most censored countries, determined by the following criteria: state control of the media, formal censorship rules, violence against and imprisonment of journalists, and restricted access to foreign news and the Internet.
The Committee to Protect Journalists, New York, 2006

| North Korea | Burma | Turkmenistan | Equatorial Guinea | Libya | Eritrea | Cuba | Uzbekistan | Syria | Belarus |

I am happy ▾

% of population

Percentage of population stated that they were 'very happy'.
World Values Survey, 1981-2004

Venezuela	Nigeria	Iceland Ireland	Philippines Netherlands	United States Australia/Turkey	United Kingdom Switzerland	Belgium	Sweden Denmark	Canada Dominican Republic	Mexico
55	45	42	40	39	38	37	36	32	31

↑ Another filter offers different world statistics of potential collective interest, such as "What nation's people are most censored?" or "How happy are people around the world?"

What did you learn from the process that you didn't expect?

GS: The world filled up so quickly! Most European countries were represented on the map after two weeks. Six months after project launch, Africa is blank. We're waiting for the first visitor from the Vatican.

What insights occur by presenting data in graphic rather than non-graphic form?

GS: Site traffic is usually summarized with complex statistics shown in table format. A tabular list of data is abstract. Collections of data can be shown visually to crystallize the meaning of complex data. Users leave a visual trace on our website, and can watch the traces of other people around the world. It is like moving your finger on a globe and imagining a world trip.

Showing How You Digg It

Design Firm
Digg/Stamen Design

Project
Content Visualization

Client
Digg Labs

Q&A with
Kevin Rose, Digg Founder

With the Web's overwhelming array of information, sites that offer meaningful ways of finding and rating content are giving users shelter in the storm—and a way to access and share the things in which they are most interested. Digg.com is an online destination where users submit and rate content from sources all over the Web. Digg Labs creates visual tools designed to give people a broader, deeper, and visually interesting view of the content on Digg.com.

↑ Digg Arc displays stories, topics, and other Web content wrapped around a sphere.

How did Digg Labs come about?

KR: Digg Labs began with the Digg Spy data visualization, developed as a real-time way to view data as it came into Digg.com. With Spy, we saw intriguing patterns in the data. Spy inspired us to invent other ways to visually represent activity on Digg to surface other meaningful patterns in how people are viewing and sharing content. We had heard rumors about Stamen Design creating innovative data visualizations. We explored ideas with them, which led to Stack, our first visualization with Stamen.

What is Digg Labs' mission?

KR: Our projects let users explore activity beneath the surface of the Digg community. Visualizations identify patterns on Digg and give users different ways to interact and see what other people find interesting.

"We regard the visualizations as more of a science experiment than an artistic endeavor." —Kevin Rose

The Digg Stack visualization shows how users rate content in real time and displays data on up to 100 stories at once. Site users' ("Diggers") names fall from above and stack above popular stories. Brightly colored stories have more Diggs.

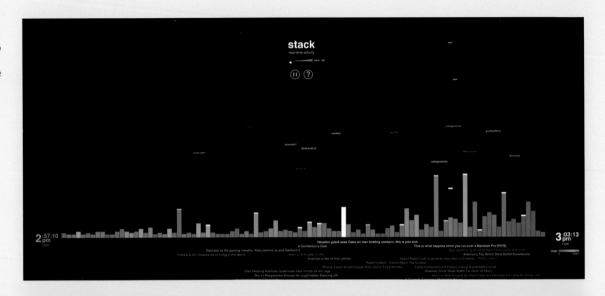

Digg Swarm draws a circle around stories as users read and rate them. As Diggers swarm around/interact with particular stories, the stories grow. Brightly colored stories have more Diggs.

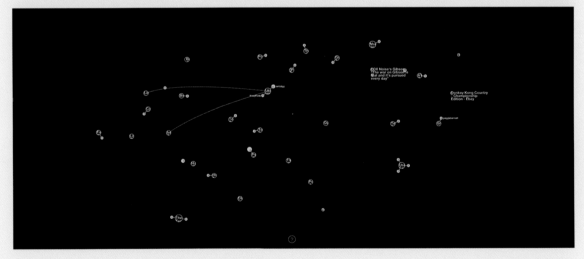

Describe the concepts behind the visualization models Arc, BigSpy, Stack, and Swarm.

KR: Stack represents stories on a timeline and is useful for watching the volume of Digg activity in relation to story popularity over time. With Swarm, you can watch the interaction between users and stories. We wanted to see how users moved between stories, and Swarm highlights these relationships. BigSpy provides a visually compelling version of the simple HTML Spy. Arc is a dynamic pie chart of activity across different sections of the site and shows which topics are most active, and how the community is Digging content across topics.

Besides being cool, what do you think these visualizations do for the user experience that's different/better than traditional methods?

KR: We regard the visualizations as more of a science experiment than an artistic endeavor, not to underestimate their visual appeal. The visualizations draw out connections and relationships that someone may not recognize or appreciate in the traditional list view. Interesting stories come to your attention that you may not otherwise have noticed.

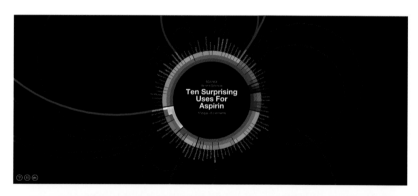

Digg Arc visualizes site activity as users "Digg" stories across topics. Stories with more "Diggs" make thicker arcs in the visualization.

As users rate stories, Digg BigSpy places story headlines at the top of the screen. As new stories drop down from the top of the screen, older stories shift down on the list. More popular stories have titles displayed in larger type.

Running the Numbers

Artist
Chris Jordan

Project
**Running the Numbers:
An American Self Portrait**

Q&A with
Chris Jordan

Chris Jordan portrays contemporary American culture through the austere lens of statistics. Depicting specific quantities of everyday objects, Jordan's work elevates numbers from the realm of statistics and places them into a more dramatic context. When we can see what fifteen million sheets of office paper (equal to five minutes of paper use in the United States) looks like, we begin to understand our personal impact on the world with a fresh perspective.

"I realized that if I could escape some of the limitations of straight photography, I could use a combination of photography and digital processing to depict the actual quantities of things in a way that cannot be done any other way."

—Chris Jordan

What is your process for creating each piece?

CJ: I start with a powerful or shocking statistic, and imagine ways of visually depicting it. I sketch and experiment a lot before I settle on a concept with the complexity I'm looking for. Then I take many photographs of the subject (a small pile of cell phones, for example) and stitch them together into a single huge image. That way I keep track of the amounts and ensure that I'm accurately depicting the statistic, as well as creating a photographic image that doesn't exist in reality.

How do you hope people will react to the work?

CJ: I work with themes that are meant to inspire reflection about the role of the individual in our mass culture. My big prints invite the viewer up close, where they can see the small details comprising the whole. This experience of one/many and near/far hopefully causes the viewer to consider their place in our incomprehensibly enormous society. My ultimate goal is to help the viewer connect with their sense of mattering in the world.

Have you been surprised by response to the work?

CJ: Public response to my Running the Numbers series has been astonishing. A new consciousness is spreading around the globe, like fresh grass growing up through an old cracked parking lot. Thinkers and visionaries are talking and writing books about it. People who connect with this movement also tend to connect with my work. It is an inspiring process to be a part of.

↑ *Plastic Bottles* is a 60 x 120-inch (152 x 304.8 cm) digital photograph depicting two million plastic beverage bottles (see detail at right), the number used in the U.S. every five minutes.

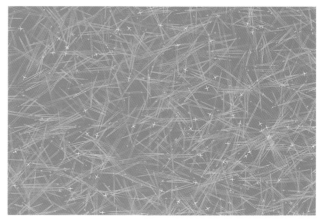

↑ *Jet Trails* is a 60 x 96-inch (152 x 244 cm) digital photograph depicting 11,000 jet trails (see detail at right), equal to the number of commercial flights in the U.S. every eight hours.

Similar Diversity

Designers
**Philipp Steinweber
and Andreas Koller**

Project
Similar Diversity

Q&A with
**Philipp Steinweber
and Andreas Koller**

Designers Phillipp Steinweber and Andreas Koller organized their Similar Diversity project around holy texts to create visual and conceptual connections between the different world religions. The information graphic is essentially a data visualization of the Holy Books of five world religions showing the commonalities and differences of Christianity, Islam, Hinduism, Buddhism, and Judaism. The goal: Offer viewers fresh insight into the topics of religion and faith.

The designers experimented with several different visualization methods and ways of presentation, but eventually chose the arc motif because of its graphic appeal.

How did this project come about?

AK: Similar Diversity was created in the context of a workshop with Stefan Sagmeister. The topic: "Is it possible to touch someone's heart with design?" The project's aim was to touch not just one heart but also "the whole world." We chose the topic of religion, which reaches so many people. We were both interested in data visualization, so we decided to visualize the text of the Holy Books.

What drove design decisions for the project?

PS: Our goal is to inspire viewers to think about their own prejudices and religious conflicts. We tried to show complex connections in a simple way, while still communicating depth.

Why visually represent the work as a wall diagram rather than another media format?

AK: The details did not translate well in a smaller format. We are working on posters. We considered digital representation, but haven't had time to implement it the way we'd want to. Perhaps one day we'll create an online version.

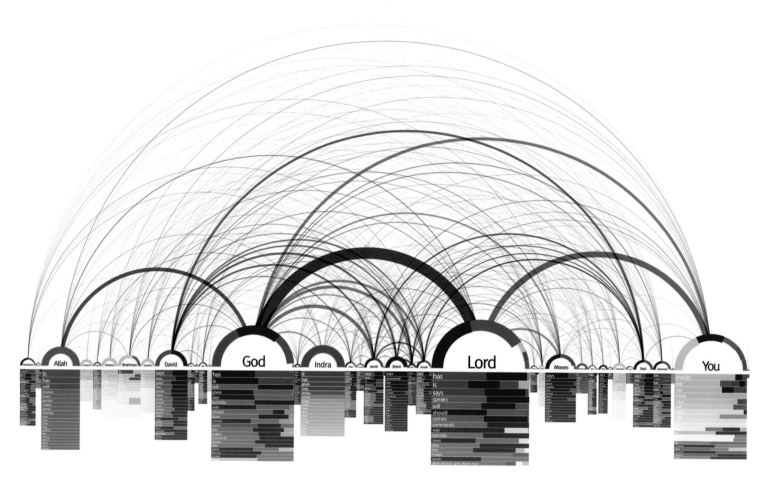

The main graphic for the Similar Diversity project shows the forty-one most frequent characters from different Holy Texts and their commonalities. Character names appear alphabetically on the x-axis. The size of the names and arcs are calculated from the total word count in all scriptures. The colored segments of the arcs show the frequency of the word representing the character in the respective texts.

Viewers explore the Similar
Diversity graphic in the gallery.

A photographic detail of the
upper part of the visualization
shows the interconnecting arcs,
which represent the relationships between characters from
the different Holy Texts. Each
arc's thickness is calculated by an
algorithmic formula based on the
frequency of any given activity that
a connected pair of characters per-
forms in the written material.

What did you learn from the process that you didn't expect?

PS: We were astonished by the complexity of the visualization process, despite the
fact that we were working with simple data (text only). It was challenging to bring
these structures into an organized graphic.

**What emotional, intellectual, or spiritual insights occur when people absorb the
piece that might not otherwise occur if the data was presented in a nonvisual form?**

AK: The connections and commonalities between different Holy Books become obvious.
Hopefully the work provokes people to think about the absurdity of current religious
conflicts by giving them a closer look at a topic they might not read a long text about.

What surprised you about how people respond to the information?

PS: The amount of interest in discussing religious and interrelated world political
issues in this context was astounding.

This detail from the main Similar
Diversity graphic shows a bar
chart breakdown of one character's activities in the respective
Holy Texts.

Viewing Private Worlds

Designers
**Jonathan Harris and
Sep Kamvar**

Project
**User-submitted
Content Experience**

Q&A
Jonathan Harris

Designer Jonathan Harris' two projects, We Feel Fine and the Yahoo! Time Capsule, offer insight into the diverse and intriguing mix of humanity online. Social networking, blogging, IM, message boards, and content-sharing tools have turned the Web into a gateway to even the most minute details of the human experience. Harris' work engagingly captures private thoughts and feelings as well as content and ideas from online users around the world.

> **"In my work, I try to satisfy three basic goals: a universally understandable concept, simplicity of execution, and playfulness."**
>
> —Jonathan Harris

How did the idea for We Feel Fine come about?

JH: People are keeping blogs, posting photographs—leaving behind digital footprints telling stories of their lives. My collaborator, Sep Kamvar, and I wanted to unearth this hidden humanity in a beautiful way.

What were the challenges and surprises in designing We Feel Fine?

JH: In my work, I try to ensure that the way something is represented also matches its nature. In We Feel Fine, the colored particles exhibit traits like curiosity, fright, and euphoria. The particles can also self-organize along any number of axes to provide statistical insights into the world's feelings. The micro and macro work together to make We Feel Fine successful.

How did the idea of the time capsule come about?

JH: Yahoo! contacted me with the idea of creating a world time capsule for 2006. I suggested organizing this time capsule around ten universal themes (like love, sadness, and hope), each of which would have a single simple question ("What do you love?" or "What makes you sad?"). People could respond to the questions with words, drawings, pictures, video, and sound.

BEAUTY
17157

PAST
10899

NOW
11847

FAITH
9328

HOPE
14560

SORROW
6352

YOU
16617

FUN
16634

LOVE
44758

ANGER
3391

The Yahoo! Time Capsule was visualized as a spinning globe, the surface of which was entirely composed of the words and pictures that people had submitted. Clicking any spot on the globe would cause the globe to unwrap into filmstrips, allowing people to browse the individual stories composing the globe.

What were the challenges and surprises of designing the Time Capsule?

JH: The interface had to work in many languages, so words were kept to a minimum, making a primarily visual experience.

Was the response to the Time Capsule as expected?

JH: The Time Capsule collected hundreds of thousands of stories from people all across the world. In contrast to the raw and intensely revealing stories in We Feel Fine, the stories submitted to the Time Capsule were tame, often verging on cliché. We Feel Fine uses a technique I call "passive observation," meaning that it passively observes people living their lives (which is hard to fake). The Time Capsule asks direct questions, which influences the way people respond.

Now that the Internet has an abundance of social networking sites and peer-driven online communities, what are the benefits of creating a "walled garden" experience?

JH: My work provides windows into small areas of life. After creating enough windows, a picture of the world emerges, adding insights and spotting patterns that can be difficult to see from within the teeming chaos.

"**People are moved by the candor and sincerity of their fellow humans. It's not often that we get to witness strangers in these private moments.**" —Jonathan Harris

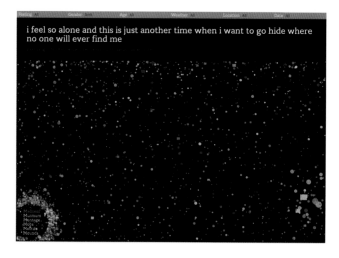

"I noticed that the Web, commonly considered to be a cold, inhuman space, was actually harboring a huge amount of humanity," explains Harris.

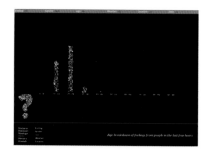

We Feel Fine allows people to explore how other people are feeling all over the world. This data can be filtered by a number of criteria, including age, geographic location, and climate.

Analyzing Wikipedia

Wikipedia, a peer-created information source, is one of the most often-cited online reference resources. Constantly created and edited collaboratively by millions of users worldwide, it has been widely criticized, especially by those in the library science field, for its inaccuracies. Three members of the School of Library and Information Science's Information Visualization Lab at Indiana University created an online mosaic illustrating Wikipedia's editing trends.

Designers
**Bruce William Herr III,
Todd Holloway, and
Dr. Katy Börner**

Project
**Wikipedia Activity
Visualization**

Q&A with
**Bruce William Herr III,
Todd Holloway, and
Dr. Katy Börner**

"Accuracy and activity are intertwined in Wikipedia, partially because topics of high activity are self-repairing." —Todd Holloway

What prompted the idea to analyze Wikipedia activity?

KB: We wanted to analyze the structure of Wikipedia. The structure, with the links between pages, is visually encoded by the layout of nodes and images. We decided to reveal revision activity (with color and size encodings of the nodes) both because it might add to the debate about the pros and cons of Wikipedia's collaborative architecture, and because it helps explain how the structure arose.

How did you determine the visual approach for the project?

BH: One approach to visualizing Wikipedia's structure is to first say that two pages in Wikipedia are similar if they are linked from many of the same pages. Then an algorithm is used to plot similar pages near one another, and dissimilar ones apart. We did that and then expanded on the technique by introducing representative images in the background, and layering additional information (revision activity) that helps explain the underlying structure.

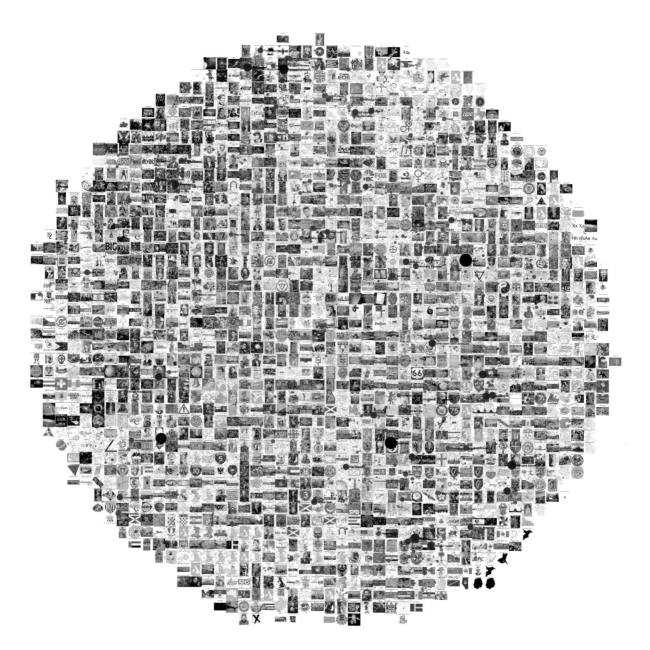

The Wikipedia Activity mosaic measures 5 x 5 feet (1.52 x 1.52 m) in printed form.

Wikipedia and other peer-created information sources have been criticized for not being accurate despite wide usage. What do you think about that and how do tools like yours contribute to the conversation?

TH: Accuracy and activity are intertwined in Wikipedia, partially because topics of high activity are self-repairing—someone, somewhere will always quickly fix mistakes or vandalism—and partially because topics of high activity potentially indicate division of viewpoints.

Macro perspectives such as our visualization provide many revelations about such activity. For example, the region of pages devoted to mathematics in the lower left corner of our visualization is quite dense—indicating that many pages are highly interlinked. Obviously there are few pages in this region with high revision activity, perhaps indicating maturity of the content and high accuracy. The one exception is the page entitled "Earth," shown as a very large node for its high activity, which is likely embroiled in the global warming debate.

↑ The size of the nodes or circles on the mosaic represents the amount of revision activity on a particular Wikipedia article.

↑ Larger nodes indicate an entry with content that has been frequently updated and perhaps reveals subject matter controversy.

Contributors

Information design, as a field, is on the threshold of a unique and unprecedented convergence. We are very grateful to the outstanding practitioners who embrace both technical and aesthetic sensibilities, and who generously shared their work. This book would not have been possible without them.

"To design is much more than simply to assemble, to order, or even to edit; it is to add value and meaning, to illuminate, to simplify, to clarify, to modify, to dignify, to dramatize, to persuade, and perhaps even to amuse. To design is to transform prose into poetry."

—Paul Rand

50,000feet, Inc.
Chicago, IL
USA
773.528.6760
50000feet.com

Addison
New York, NY
USA
212.229.5000
addison.com

AIGA, the professional association for design
New York, NY
USA
212.807.1799
aiga.org

And Partners
New York, NY
USA
212.414.2915
andpartnersny.com

Applied Storytelling
Lafayette, CA
USA
925.871.3572
appliedstorytelling.com

Axis41
Salt Lake City, UT
USA
801.303.6300
axis41.com

Fernando Gómez Baptista
El Correo
Bilbao
Spain
69.692.0081

Blank Mosseri
New York, NY
USA
646.329.9606
blankmosseri.com

Boag Associates Ltd.
London
UK
44.20.3008.6491
boag.co.uk

Bureau Mijksenaar
Amsterdam
The Netherlands
31.20.409.0244
mijksenaar.com

Carbone Smolan Agency
New York, NY
USA
212.807.0077
carbonesmolan.com

Cheng Design
Seattle, WA
USA
206.328.4047
cheng-design.com

Sonia Chia
Rhode Island
School of Design
Providence, RI
USA

K.J. Chun
Seattle, WA
USA
206.623.1044
methodologie.com

Communication Research Institute
Australia
61.394.898.640
communication.org.au

Crazy Egg, Inc.
USA
714.398.8373
crazyegg.com

Design Army
Washington, DC
USA
202.797.1018
designarmy.com

Digg
San Francisco, CA
USA
digg.com

Fauxpas Grafik
Zürich
Switzerland
41.43.333.1105
fauxpas.ch

Forsman & Bodenfors
Gothenburg
Sweden
46.31.17.6730
fb.se

frog design
Palo Alto, CA
USA
650.856.3764
frogdesign.com

Frost Design
Sydney
Australia
61.2.9280.4233
frostdesign.com.au

Funnel Incorporated
Middleton, WI
USA
608.213.8144
funnelinc.com

Guerrini Design Island
Buenos Aires
Argentina
54.11.4315.8433
guerriniisland.com

Headcase Design
Philadelphia, PA
USA
215.922.5393
headcasedesign.com

Hello Design
Culver City, CA
USA
310.839.4885
hellodesign.com

Bruce William Herr III,
Todd Holloway, and
Dr. Katy Börner
Indiana University
Department of
Computer Science
Bloomington, IN
USA
abeautifulwww.com

Nigel Holmes
Westport, CT
USA
203.226.2313
nigelholmes.com

Hunt Design
Pasadena, CA
USA
626.793.7847
huntdesign.com

Hybrid Design
San Francisco, CA
USA
415.227.4700
hybrid-design.com

Imaginary Forces
Los Angeles, CA
USA
323.957.6868
imaginaryforces.com

Infinite Scale Design Group
Salt Lake City, UT
USA
801.363.1881
infinitescale.com

InfoGraphics
New York, NY
USA
infog.com

Information Design Studio
Amsterdam
The Netherlands
31.20.489.3081
theworldasflatland.net

johnson banks
London
UK
44.207.587.6400
johnsonbanks.co.uk

Chris Jordan
Seattle, WA
USA
206.706.1550
chrisjordan.com

Kahn + Associates
Paris
France
33.01.4454.2224
kahnplus.com

KBDA
Los Angeles, CA
USA
310.255.0902
kbda.com

Kolegram/Iridium
Gatineau, Québec
Canada
819.777.5538
kolegram.com

Krzysztof Lenk
Rhode Island
School of Design
Providence, RI
USA

Landesberg Design
Pittsburgh, PA
USA
412.381.2220
landesbergdesign.com

Harmen Liemburg
Amsterdam
The Netherlands
31.62.508.0766
harmenliemburg.nl

Liska + Associates
Chicago, IL
USA
312.644.4400
liska.com

Louise Sandhaus Design/
Durfee Regn Sandhaus
Los Angeles, CA
USA
323.667.2039
lsd-studio.net

William Lutz
Rutgers University
Camden, NJ
USA
wlutz@camden.rutgers.edu

Matter
Atlanta, GA
USA
404.961.2060
matterco.com

McMillan
Ottawa, ON
Canada
613.789.1234
thinkmcmillan.com

MetaDesign
San Francisco, CA
USA
415.627.0790
metadesign.com

Method
San Francisco, CA
USA
415.901.6300
method.com

Metro Design Studio
Los Angeles, CA
USA
213.922.2346
metro.net

The *New York Times*
Graphics Department
New York, NY
USA
nytimes.com

Number 27
Brooklyn, NY
USA
number27.org

Olson Kotowski, Inc.
Torrance, CA
USA
olsonkotowski.com

Open
New York, NY
USA
212.645.5633
notclosed.com

Pentagram Design
New York, NY
USA
212.683.7000
pentagram.com

Planet Propaganda
Madison, WI
USA
608.256.0000
planetpropaganda.com

Poulin + Morris, Inc.
New York, NY
USA
212.675.1332
poulinmorris.com

Push Design
Seattle, WA
USA
206.749.9995
pushdesign.net

Ralph Appelbaum
Associates
New York, NY
USA
212.334.8200
RAANY.com

Rethink
Vancouver, BC
Canada
604.685.8911

Rutka Weadock Design
Baltimore, MD
USA
410.563.2100
rutkaweadock.com

Saatchi & Saatchi LA
Torrance, CA
USA
310.214.6000
saatchi.com

Sagmeister Inc.
New York, NY
USA
212.647.1789
sagmeister.com

Satellite Design
San Francisco, CA
USA
415.371.1610
satellite-design.com

Second Story
Interactive Studios
Portland, OR
USA
503.827.7155
secondstory.com

Simon & Goetz Design
Frankfurt
Germany
49.69.968.883
simongoetz.de

Smart Design
New York, NY
USA
212.807.8150
smartdesignworldwide.com

Philipp Steinweber
and Andreas Koller
contact@similardiversity.net
similardiversity.net

Sullivan
New York, NY
USA
212.888.2881
sullivannyc.com

Robert Swinehart
Carnegie Mellon University
Pittsburgh, PA
USA

thomas.matthews
London
England
44.20.7403.4281
thomasmatthews.com

Alejandro Tumas,
Pablo Loscri, and
Javier Vera Ocampo
Buenos Aires
Argentina
atumas@clarin.com

Jill Vacarra Design
Santa Monica, CA
USA
jill@jillvacarra.com

The *Wall Street Journal*
Information Graphics Staff
New York, NY
USA
212.416.2797

What's Next
Interactive Inc.
Redondo Beach, CA
USA
whatsnextinteractive.com

White Rhino
Burlington, MA
USA
781.270.4545
whiterhino.com

Vanderbyl Design
San Francisco, CA
USA
415.543.8447
vanderbyl.com

VSA Partners, Inc.
Chicago, IL
USA
312.427.6413

Zagnoli McEvoy Foley LLC
Chicago, IL
USA
zmf.com

ABOUT THE AUTHOR

Kim Baer, principal of Los Angeles–based design studio KBDA, developed a very early interest in graphic design as a way to integrate three distinct passions: an enthusiasm for exploring diverse types of organizations, a love for the written word, and an unshakable confidence in design's ability to get audiences to sit up and take notice.

Over the years, KBDA has hosted a diverse creative team, schooled in graphic design, writing, photography, architecture, boat-building, interior design, filmmaking, engineering, biology, fundraising, and rock and roll. KBDA and its extended family have leveraged these talents to create strategic work across a host of disciplines.

Consistently honored by every major design and business organization in the country, KBDA has produced work that has been featured in the Library of Congress and regularly published in numerous design compilations. National design magazines, including *Communication Arts, Print, Graphis, STEP,* and *HOW,* have consistently showcased the firm's work and methodology.

Kim Baer frequently judges design competitions and speaks at conferences across the country. She received the Fellows Award from the Los Angeles chapter of the American Institute of Graphic Arts (AIGA) in honor of lifetime achievement.

WITH MANY THANKS

Every project at KBDA is extremely collaborative, and this book is a great example. It would not have come to pass without some incredibly talented people. This includes Jill Vacarra, who helped with the structure and writing; Keith Knueven and Allison Bloss, who created and continually refined the design; Leslie Lewis and Jenny Ford, who worked to make it all happen; and Elizabeth Salud, who did an extraordinary job gathering images from around the world while helping with so many of the design decisions.

With unending thanks to Michael, who patiently waited for it all to be finished.

RESOURCES

Reference Books

Abrams, J. & Hall, P. (2006) *Elsewhere: Mapping.* Minneapolis, MN: University of Minnesota Press

Lipton, R. (2007) *The Practical Guide to Information Design.* Hoboken, NJ: John Wiley & Sons, Inc.

Mijksenaar, P. (1997) *Visual Function.* New York, NY: Princeton Architectural Press

Saffer, D. (2007) *Designing for Interaction.* Indianapolis, IN: New Riders

Schriver, K. A. (1997) *Dynamics in Document Design.* New York, NY: John A. Wiley

Shedroff, N. (2001) *Experience Design.* Indianapolis, IN: New Riders

Spiekermann, E. and Ginger, E. M. (1993) *Stop Stealing Sheep.* Mountain View, CA: Adobe Press

Tufte, E. S. (2006) *Beautiful Evidence.* Cheshire, CT: Graphics Press

Tufte, E. S. (1990) *Envisioning Information.* Cheshire, CT: Graphics Press

Tufte, E. S. (1983) *The Visual Display of Quantitative Information* (2nd Ed.). Cheshire, CT: Graphics Press

Tufte, E. S. (1997) *Visual Explanations.* Cheshire, CT: Graphics Press

Wurman, R. S. (1989) *Information Anxiety.* New York, NY: Doubleday

Wurman, R. S. (1996) *Information Architects.* New York, NY: Graphis Press

Jacobsen, R. (2000) *Information Design.* Cambridge, MA: MIT Press

Sites & Online Journals

International Institute for Information Design
iiid.net

Info Design: Understanding by Design
informationdesign.org

Information Design: Professional Resources: AIGA
aiga.org/content.cfm/clear

Information Design Journal
benjamins.com/cgi-bin/t_seriesview.cgi?series=idj